A Country Diary

A COUNTRY DIARY

Selected from the Guardian
by *Jeannette Page*

With a Foreword by
Melvyn Bragg

FOURTH ESTATE · *London*

First published in Great Britain in 1994 by
Fourth Estate Limited
289 Westbourne Grove
London W11 2QA

A catalogue record for this book is available from the
British Library.

ISBN 1–85702–254–8

Designed by Fielding Rowinski
Typeset by York House Typographic Ltd
Printed in Great Britain by Biddles Ltd, Guildford and King's Lynn

CONTENTS

FOREWORD

I would guess that for many people "A Country Diary" is one of their touchstones of sanity. In a world bound fast in a new ice age of technology and bureaucracy, it brings us a truth disguised as the unexpected. Byways, green shoots, lonely tarns, curious flockings and visitings. We have daily evidence that there is still not only country but A Country outside the maw and Mammon of the nation.

Sometimes I think that it is wholly subversive.

Those who write "A Country Diary" are like the network of beacons which plotted the land at the time of the Spanish Armada. In hill country and on flat lands, and in the ruins of old hill-forts, there they glow. The writers are the quiet chorus saying, "Life is really like this, you know; it is crab apples and mist on a mountain, it is saving a village shop and knowing a rare plant. Take heart."

It is a mistake, I think, to see "A Country Diary" as nostalgic. A close reading shows it to be minutely attentive to the fluctuations of the great forces which shape the planet. Nostalgia is too short-term for that.

Although naturally environmentalist, there is little sentimental conservationalism. What the diarists tell us is that a steady look at the world of nature will yield more than all the getting and wasting. The

A COUNTRY DIARY

"Diary" is the quiet inheritor of the radical credo of the young Wordsworth and Coleridge, who fled from Reason when it became the Terror. They sought and found in a sensual and intellectual study of nature a means and faith for life. Many nowadays recognise or long for this.

The pleasures of the "Diary" are numerous, but for me it brings a rare chance to see our islands whole. Like the shipping forecast which sails its way around the coastline, "A Country Diary" reminds us of the most salient factors in our lives: the earth we move on, the air we breathe, the natural life we live in. It is full of stealthily observed riches.

MELVYN BRAGG *1994*

INTRODUCTION

What is it about "A Country Diary" that makes many readers turn there first? Why is it that when a diarist misses his or her slot, the phone and post buzz with inquiries?

The "Diary" provides a calm entry into another day battling with traffic, crowds, the ever faster pace of life. When you open a small window of the "Country Diary", in blows a breath of pure air. "A Country Diary" has appeared daily since before the First World War—the first was in November 1906—and the diarists are among the most loved of the *Guardian*'s writers. Three of our oldest diarists—in years and in service—are A. Harry Griffin, W. D. Campbell and William Condry.

A. Harry Griffin at 84 is one of the Lake District's most famous sons. He began writing and climbing when he was 17 and became a member of the Coniston Tigers—a young band who bought a wooden garage in Barrow, re-erected it at Coniston Old Hall as a climbing hut and spent long days on the fells. With him our readers have walked miles.

W. D. Campbell, now 88, has entertained and informed his readers, as he did his pupils, every week since 1964 with diaries about the natural history of Oxfordshire. He has not missed one week, even when he was in hospital. With him our readers have dug many gardens and watched many birds.

From Wales, William Condry—a celebrated environmentalist—has fought the country-lovers' fight in the *Guardian*'s columns for nearly 40 years. He wrote his first "Country Diary" on 9 October 1957. With him our readers have conquered mountains and protected the environment.

This collection includes contributions from Enid Wilson, a much loved and admired diarist who died on 31 July 1988. She began contributing to "A Country Diary" almost by chance in 1950 and then wrote every fortnight from Keswick. With her our readers tracked many badgers, always keeping well away from the tourist traps. In October 1992, L. P. Samuels, our diarist in Cheshire for more than 30 years, died aged 83. His essays were a delight. With him our readers kept in touch with the *Guardian*'s Manchester roots.

Now our newer diarists are reinforcing this fine tradition in their contributions from the length and breadth of the country—Wales, Scotland, Ireland, many parts of England, even London. "A Country Diary" and the diarists have a special place in the *Guardian*'s heart. In our topsy-turvy world of war, famine and greed, they keep our feet firmly on the ground. To the diarists and their followers, thank you.

JEANNETTE PAGE *1994*

SPRING

Spring

OXFORDSHIRE: Almost all of the colour in the garden at the moment, with the exception of primrose varieties and that doubtful native, the snowdrop, is of foreign origin. Some of the subjects, such as crocus and tulip species and hybrids, scillas and some early irises, have been so long-established that they are regarded as typical cottage garden plants, whilst others, such as the now ubiquitous forsythia just coming into bloom, are comparative newcomers, dating from the opening up of trade with the Far East in the middle of the last century. But, forestalling the forsythia by some weeks, the pride of place in my garden is now occupied by another yellow-flowered shrub of far superior quality—the cornelian cherry (*Cornus mas*). It has always puzzled me that although this southern European dogwood was introduced to English gardens at least 400 years ago, it has never become a "must" as the more vulgar forsythia has become for both suburban and cottage gardens.

The early blooming of myriads of tiny yellow bunches of stars on bare twigs is not the only virtue of this shrub, for eventually, when the bush is becoming almost a tree after twenty years or so, fruiting becomes regular. Here I have to declare a personal interest, for I discovered long ago, having a friend's ancient specimen at my

13

disposal, that the scarlet, almost transparent "cherries" are so thin-skinned that their succulent pulp is readily available, and greedily consumed, even by soft-billed birds such as warblers and wrens. The twenty-one-year-old specimen which I left in my last garden when I retired fruited abundantly in the following year: its offspring in my present garden just bore a few fruits last year, at about fifteen years old, and I shall be lucky if I live to see it, in some distant July or August, swarming with appreciative warblers, wrens and thrushes.

W. D. CAMPBELL *27 March 1985*

KESWICK: The end of March, the start of April, and the lawn mowers are emerging on to rather mossy lawns after one of the dampest and mildest winters for years. I do not want to start, or continue, an argument but I wish someone could tell me with any certitude how harmful, or not, moss- and weedkillers and indeed sprays are generally to the birds who feed along the lawns and elsewhere. I have noticed and commented on the declining number of small birds here for some years now. It has been said that gardens in and around towns will soon become important refuges for birds in these days of hedge and rough-land clearance. Is it true? It seems foolish to feed birds in winter and provide nest sites, and yet use perhaps doubtful products in gardens. Until about twelve years ago a whitethroat always raised broods near my nettle bed—it is still thriving—and while these birds' troubles probably lie in their wintering places, other warblers—willow, chiffchaff and garden—are fewer, too. Even chaffinches and song thrushes are less common here; indeed, only blackbirds are "common", though dunnocks, tits, wrens, or robins are much the same. Neither the resident sparrow-hawk nor the magpies can be blamed; they have usually been about for the last five years. I have used no garden chemicals (yet) and as a reward have disgracefully lichened apple trees, and a tree-creeper to enjoy them. I came home last night in a soft, damp twilight to moths at the windows and a blackbird singing itself to sleep, just as the owls began to call in the far wood. But could we, too, come to a "silent spring"? An old gardening book recommends lime wash for mossed trees, fine coal ash for the lawns and "refuse" salt for green paths. Other days, gentler ways?

ENID WILSON *28 March 1983*

OXFORDSHIRE: Once again weathermen and the media have assured us that spring began on 21 March, and again I assert that this is nonsense. I have pointed out before that each season occupies three months of the year—the quarters. If 21 March is the beginning of spring, the season will end around 21 June, which is midsummer, which suggests that the first half of summer occurs in springtime.

A few nights ago I awoke in the early hours with a vague notion that some small creature was moving in the room. I switched on the bedside light and there was a small bird circling round just beneath the ceiling. From time to time it perched on the shade of an unlit overhead light, and occasionally disappeared through the open door into the passage leading to other rooms with open doors. Yet it returned again and again but, because I could only see shape and not colour, I could not identify it; from its long tail I nearly decided that it must be a pied wagtail, but then realised that it was not large enough. The only possible point of entry was an upper window in my bedroom which was only two or three inches ajar. Finally the bird disappeared and I switched off the light and went to sleep. Next morning I searched every available room for the intruder but finding no trace almost convinced myself that I had had a very realistic dream. Two days later I found the corpse of a long-tailed tit beneath a cupboard in another room. The precise identification gave me a clue to the possible explanation for the fatal visit. Long-tailed tits methodically examine windows to search for insects and spiders along the woodwork and metal strips holding the glass, and I guess that in examining one strip which contains an open window in its centre they willy-nilly enter the room. I came to this conclusion last summer when on three occasions tits of this species were fluttering around in my glass conservatory where the only possible entrance was by a window slightly ajar. These were luckier as I caught and released them.

W. D. CAMPBELL *30 March 1994*

SPRING

THAMES TOWPATH, HAM: Whether we have the warmth of summer or cold early spring winds, the season's turn from dark to light is unstoppable. Winter flocks of chaffinches are separating to pair up for mating. Blackbirds are already busy. You see the low determined flight to some bush or other. The bird disappears, reappears with the same single-minded purpose of finding more pieces of nest-building material. Great tits are sawing out their messages of courtship, whilst the pigeons strut their stuff at any opportunity, puffed-up necks glinting like rainbows in the sun. Mallards have already produced their first brood. Ducklings dash around like mechanical toys, fussing and anxious lest the little they know of life be lost. Trees teeter on the brink of leaves. The wych-elm has tight clusters of green seeds whilst the alders are carrying catkins, some of them seven inches long. Huge willows growing on the north bank appear to throw showers of golden rain over the water as the sun reflects on the new fresh leaves and their radiance. Last year's traveller's joy is still looped over the branches with new leaves opening. This plant used to be called by some "boys' bacca" because boys smoked the dried stems. There is plenty of it here. Unexpectedly a sharp sweet song and a distinctive shape registered a warbler. A sedge-warbler was announcing his unusually early arrival with clarity and grace. The other delights were more expected. A peacock butterfly landed on the path in front of us sporting a newly minted smartness as if the months of hibernation had been spent in deep happiness. The nettles that they prefer for their eggs are still very small. A brimstone was also patrolling along the scrub looking for a mate. She will probably rely on the buckthorns for her egg-laying. Meanwhile at home frogs surrounded by spawn sing and croon to each other through the warmth of the spring sun. Like every other living thing their enthusiasm wanes slightly when the rain falls and cold winds blow.

AUDREY INSCH *20 March 1993*

SPRING

SOMERSET: Whatever changes politicians may have in mind for May Day holidays, our village is robustly reviving ancient tradition. Leaflets advertised the "Jack-in-the-Green Sweeps' Festival". The village's own chimney-sweep was both inspiration and organiser. There was initial anxiety about the rumoured pagan origins of the event. An informative leaflet was produced from Rochester, where the sweeps festival is well established. Jack-in-the-Green, it says, appeared at dawn on May Day, at the climax of the rites of Beltane. He represented the spirit of the King sacrificed earlier, reborn by the power of the sun, which was represented by the "ban-fire". He was a symbol of resurrection and appropriated by churches at Easter when the Jack—in a wooden framework festooned with greenery—was set up in the nave of the church as an allegorical figure. Outside the church, dancers round the ban-fire, with sooty faces, became an important feature of the festivities. Black-faced ("Moorish" or "Morris") dancers were then the link with chimney-sweeps, who came to be thought of as associated with new life, and lucky at weddings. Our event was faithful to the antecedents described on the Rochester leaflet. Jack-in-the-Green was authentic in his pyramid-frame. We had the Dorset Triumph Morris Dancers and Treacle Easter Clog Dancers. The children of the Templecombe primary school, in traditional dress, danced around the maypole. Entirely in the spirit of earlier festivals, though less directly significant as symbols, were the Shaftesbury Town Silver Band, lambs from Farmer Giles's Farmstead (which you could feed from a bottle), baby rabbits and old farm machinery wheezing and puffing. You could guess the name of a lamb or the weight of a very big, rather taciturn, white goat. There were ice-creams and a tea-tent. Cars lined the approach roads to the tiny village,

19

and more than 500 people had a wonderful time. It felt like a good way for Christians or people of any persuasion to celebrate new life.

JOHN VALLINS *18 May 1993*

STRATHNAIRN: Crossing the burn was not easy as although the water was nowhere near the top of my wellingtons I was carrying a large orange shopping bag filled with five bat boxes. On the banks of the crossing point there were so many flowering marsh marigolds that I could not put my foot down without treading on some of the blossoms. I scrambled up the bank and negotiated a fence whilst the ewes and lambs in the field looked on in what appeared to be amusement, or at least curiosity. My destination was a large group of old birch trees not far from the River Nairn which I hoped would attract Daubentons bats. This species of bat is also called the water bat, because of its habit of flying low over water and picking off insects, and they are even reputed to take small fish. It was difficult to find five suitable birch trees, as the main criterion was that the flight path of a bat to and from the box had to be free of any obstacle such as twigs or branches. However, the very first tree I looked at was indeed suitable and I reached up as far as I could to fix the box to the tree. Bat boxes are similar to small bird boxes in size, but instead of a hole in the side the box has a split in the base which gives access to bats. Inside the box on the back, grooves are cut to enable bats to have a better grip as they crawl in. The next box went up on a straight-trunked birch on the edge of a glade in the middle of the group of trees and this box went slightly higher as there was a convenient boulder near the base of the tree on which I could stand. I tried to erect the boxes facing in various directions, hoping that at least some of them would be suitable as a summer roost, although admittedly five boxes are not likely to drastically alter the habits of many bats in the strath. There are now hundreds of bat boxes in the Highlands, mainly erected by the Forestry Commission, and bats have even colonised boxes in pure stands of conifers.

RAY COLLIER *13 May 1993*

SOMERSET: A few weeks back, high winds snapped two big branches off the old willow that leans across the next-door millpond. This weekend the remaining members bent and groaned near breaking-point. Through the lambing season, the weather has been intermittently wet and blustery. Our neighbour with the Dartmoor grey-face flock has kept her expectant ewes in or near the shed at night so that 3 a.m. maternity calls could be made under shelter. Fourteen lambs have been born and only one lost—to a mysterious complaint. The survivors are now vigorous, lively, solid and weighty, enjoying life with their mothers in the paddock beside the house. The two original prize ewes who began the flock in 1988, Merryvale and

Tavey, seem aware of their seniority. Other names are Tor and Tamar, Dart, Drum and Drift (so called because of her snow-white fleece) and, amongst the recent generations, Caper (a lively dancer when young) and her daughter, Capability. The future prospects of each animal depend not only on gender but also on markings. To be registered as a prime specimen of the breed a lamb must have a nose that is black but not too solidly so; there should be clearly separated black spots. There must be no black except on the nose: several frisking young rams were plainly disqualified by their black knees. There must be no horns. (Some members of this otherwise hornless breed retain residual traces.) The wool must be long-stapled, lustrous and curly, but not too curly. A young ram that passes all the stringent tests will fetch a good price. Those with black knees or horns will become mutton. We joined in feeding the mothers with "Ewe-nuts" (a potent and palatable cocktail of proteins, vitamins and minerals). Then we visited the yearlings or "Hoggs" being prepared, in matching pairs, for the show season. Already their fleeces fall in long, thick, heavy tresses. With only a little instruction, you can see which are the first-choice prize-contenders and which the reserves.

JOHN VALLINS *22 March 1994*

CHESHIRE: The phone rang at about five in the evening—it was a colleague with news of a pair of ducks seen earlier that afternoon on a nearby mere which he had identified as garganey. This is a scarce, although annual passage migrant in Cheshire; but more to the point, it was the first record of the bird in our local area. I put aside all thoughts of the evening meal, picked up my binoculars, loaded the telescope

into the car and headed towards the mere in question. I eventually made my way down the rough track which skirted one side of the stretch of water, but before reaching the first vantage point I was joined by a fellow birdwatcher and his wife—the news had travelled fast. Together we decided to keep to the track, rather than walk along the water's edge, to avoid disturbing the birds and possibly causing them to fly off. The sky was beginning to cloud over and looked distinctly threatening, consequently the light was deteriorating rapidly. The only birds visible on the open water were a pair of great crested grebes, and a closer look through the telescopes enabled us to see into the more gloomy areas under the overhanging shrubs, but still no sign of the garganey. It was beginning to look as though the birds had already departed, and we had almost completed a circular scan of the mere when another birdwatcher came down the track, climbed the stile and walked straight down towards the water's edge. Then the birds appeared, took to the air, circled round, made one attempt to land, thought better of it and disappeared over the trees behind us. Fortunately the male garganey is quite distinctive in summer plumage, having a broad white band extending from eye to nape, and a pale blue forewing which shows up well in flight. I was happy with what I had seen, and as the rain started I made my way home to an early supper.

J. M. THOMPSON *11 May 1993*

THORPE HAMLET, NORWICH: May is about the best time to find one of Britain's most attractive common butterflies, the orange tip. This species, unlike the other four common members of the Pierid or White family (to which the orange tip belongs), has only a single generation of adults in one calendar year. It emerges in late April and is on the wing only until the end of June, a period of little more than eight weeks. The male of this predominantly white insect is unmistakable because of the two prominent orange patches at the tip of the forewing—a feature that gives the butterfly the appearance of having been dipped in orange paint. The female, however, lacks such prominent distinguishing marks and could be said to resemble superficially a small or green-veined white, a misidentification that can easily be corrected once she lands, for then the distinctive green marbling on the underside of the hindwing is visible. The individual that I saw in the garden was a good fresh male, feeding among an area of garlic mustard, one of two favoured food plants (the other being lady's smock). Their predilection for the second of these two flowers means that orange tips are often found in exposed and damp meadows, where the blustery conditions of early May can offer them a real test of stamina. Yet despite its small size and fluttering action, the species has a fairly strong and rapid flight. Orange tips' dependence upon two early-flowering members of the crucifer (cabbage) family has determined, in addition to the time of the adults' emergence, much about the appearance of the eggs, larvae and pupae. The caterpillars are slender and pale green with white side-markings, making them remarkably similar to the stems and seed pods on which they feed; pupae, on the other hand, turn increasingly brown, a colour change mirrored in the seed pods as they wither in autumn.

MARK COCKER *10 May 1993*

A COUNTRY DIARY

NORTHUMBERLAND: With the car being serviced we took the village bus to Newcastle Town Moor to see the Morris dancers perform on May Day. They started performing at five in the morning, but our public transport did not allow for such an early start and with a thick mist shrouding the garden when I let the dogs out at seven o'clock, I doubt if the performers got much of an audience at their first session. As usual the forty-five-seater bus carried three passengers and we all sat near the front to swap news. It is important to make use of this service. Without support, the village bus, mobile library and shop will be lost, as most countryfolk now have their own vehicles. The drive gave a good view of farmers' and gardeners' progress; some of our hedgerows are as high as a man's shoulder, which make them impossible for a car driver to see through. Approaching the hamlet of Ogle, we crawled to a halt to let a pair of dithering partridges make up their minds to leave the grit on the tarmac for the security of the hedgerow and a hundred yards on a party of young rabbits scattered in alarm. The sight of the prancing Morris dancers dressed in white with ribbons and bells on their clothes is about as English as you can get. Yet the origins of Morris dancing are found in medieval Spain. In its original form it was performed by the Moors or "Moriscos", who occupied the country for so long. It blended with existing tradition when it became associated with the spring festivities of May. At the end of the last century there was a revival in Morris as part of heightened interest in English traditions. The music used for Morris dancing differs in various parts of the country but there seems to be freedom in using old popular song tunes as well as the few undoubtedly genuine Morris tunes.

VERONICA HEATH 7 *May 1993*

SPRING

MACHYNLLETH: The blue sky of Tuesday morning was enough to send me off on a wild-goose chase. Just the day, I told myself, to see a goshawk if ever I'm going to. This was something I would never have dreamed of doing until very recent years, because before then the goshawk was extremely rare. But the falconers have changed all that. They love goshawks and by getting them from abroad and releasing them into the British wilds, they have now established a fair-sized breeding population here. Sadly the goshawk is not much of a birdwatcher's bird. You can spend a whole day in goshawk country and never get a glimpse of one. They pass much of the day hidden in evergreen trees and usually don't come out until hunger forces them to make a quick dash for prey. Then they quickly slip back into cover. The books say your best hope of seeing a goshawk is in March when a pair may perform a spectacular display flight over their nesting site. And the best place to make for is the great big spread of conifer plantations. That is where I went on Tuesday. I left my car in a lay-by among the spruces and set off on foot, keeping to open places wherever possible to give myself wide views of the skies. Fortunately the plantations I was walking through had prospects all round because large blocks of conifers have lately been clear-felled and the trees planted in their place are still very small. I wish I could end my story by describing the exciting aerial performance put on specially for me by a pair of goshawks. The truth is I walked for hours and saw hardly a bird of any sort. Yet the quest was hugely enjoyable. The sun shone all morning; there was the music of the wind in the trees; and the hills to the north were beautifully patterned with the remains of last week's snows. Why should I ask for more?

WILLIAM CONDRY *13 March 1993*

WENSLEYDALE and TEESDALE: April was wet. Torrential downpours turned small upland trickles into foaming, peat-stained cascades. With the rain streaming down the windows and the garden awash with puddles, we decided to adopt a positive attitude to British spring weather and visit some of the best local waterfalls. The first stop was Wensleydale's Hardraw Force, which is reputed to be the highest above-ground waterfall in England but is sometimes reduced to a disappointing dribble during dry spells. It left our ears ringing from the concussion of thousands of tons of falling water, amplified by the natural amphitheatre carved by the falls. Further down the dale Aysgarth Falls are a popular attraction whatever the weather, but at this time of year the beautiful hazel coppice on the north side of the Ure steals the show, with a carpet of celandines, wood anemones, violets, primroses, dog's mercury and wild arum extending as far as the eye can see. We finished the tour at High Force, Teesdale's most famous waterfall. High Force has only been a shadow of its former self since the Cow Green dam was built above Cauldron Snout, regulating part of the Force's water supply, but it's still one of the most picturesque sights on the Tees. The rain moderated to showers and then watery sunlight, so we sat at the top of the sheer cliffs on the south bank of the

Tees, in the shelter of a forest of junipers, to watch the near suicidal aerobatics of courting lapwings. This is a rare place, a natural, pure woodland of one of our three native conifers. The juniper trees never reach more than about a hundred feet tall, but form an impenetrable thicket that offers shelter and safety for animals ranging from lizards to woodcock. It has always been a hunting ground for botanists in search of plants like the lemon-scented fern, whose citrus aroma is as unmistakable as the gin-scented juniper; I can never pass either without crushing a leaf and taking a sniff.

PHIL GATES *6 May 1993*

OXFORDSHIRE: I am unable to venture further than my garden but almost daily I have found incidents of interest. The paved area is covered with cushions of aubrietia, varying from deep purple to paler pinks and mauves, whilst alyssum (*A. montanta*) adds patches of bright yellow. But my rose hedge, now with reddish-pink opening foliage, is of especial interest because of its cheap origin. When I came here to a practically barren half-acre of ground, one of my first purchases was of bush roses, including *rosa moyesii* and *R. rubrifolia*. The latter flourished, and was cherished for its reddish foliage rather than its small pink single blooms. Its hips, small and insignificantly coloured, were produced in their thousands, and as they withered and fell, the ground was smothered with them. I had always thought that passage through a bird's digestive system was necessary for germination of the undigested seeds; this did not seem to be so with *R. rubrifolia* (now re-christened *R. glauca*) for on the ground below in the following spring, seedlings were coming up as thick as mustard and cress. I pricked out a

29

boxful, which eventually formed a ninety-foot-long hedge, and only one plant, with more vigorous growth and green leaves, was a "rogue" not true to type. Similar reproductiveness beneath the parents, has occurred with another favourite, *rosa moyesii*, which in addition to large bright red single flowers is worth growing for its autumn show of large bottle-shaped orange-red hips. But my single yellow Canary Bird (a variety of Korean *rosa xanthina*) is a treasure and a disappointment. Its early ferny foliage would make it worth growing, but since mid-April my large bush has been smothered in large single yellow roses. The disappointment is that I have not seen a single seedling. Another reminder of the good old days is a fine specimen of the bird-cherry, now in full bloom, growing through the dull sallow whose catkins are now over. This was a tiny seedling found on the edge of Loch Rannoch.

W. D. CAMPBELL *11 May 1994*

THE LAKE DISTRICT: Old men with walking sticks, young children in gym shoes and even babies cocooned in fathers' rucksacks were on top of Catbells the other day and, in their dozens, wandering along the lazy ridge to High Spy. It was a perfect day for idling on the tops—warm and sunny, barely a breath of wind and matchless views to far horizons. The last drifts of snow were still clinging to the top of the north face of Helvellyn and later, from High Spy, we saw the last white handkerchiefs of winter on Great Gable. Catbells has always seemed, to me, a family hill for enthusiasts of all ages but mostly for children; it was, I recall, my daughter's first "mountain", ticked off at the age of two and a half. A pretty name for a child's mountain—the

hill where Beatrix Potter's Mrs Tiggy-Winkle had some of her adventures, finally disappearing through a door somewhere Newlands way. And from the top, this bright afternoon, Keswick looked a fairy town in a magic landscape and Derwentwater, spread out below us like a pond, ringed with wooded fells and dotted with enchanted islands with white yachts becalmed as if floating butterflies, an exciting place for youthful adventure. We had to dawdle; there was so much to see and admire—the lovely, unspoiled Vale of Newlands and every step of the routes up Robinson and Hindscarth, the crumpled ram's-horn shape of the summit of Causey Pike and its exciting ridge, the crowded woodlands and crags of Borrowdale with sixty years of adventurous memories and, straight ahead a glimpse of the highest land in England. Two jet aircraft streaked, in a sudden crash of sound, through the Jaws of Borrowdale below on our left and a pair of ravens, as always up here, performed aerobatics for us high above the perch of High Spy. We came down by Hause Gate, past the memorial seat for Hugh Walpole, who lived in the lovely house, today carpeted with daffodils, on the lower slope of the fell looking out across the lake.

31

Each morning, after breakfast, he would cross the lawn to his big library over the garage and write quickly, often describing scenes he could see from his windows, so that many of his heroes strode these grassy slopes or ran up through the bracken and the heather to watch the sun setting behind Grasmere.

A. HARRY GRIFFIN *3 May 1993*

CHESHIRE: At last the spring butterflies have started to appear, not in any great quantity, but individuals have been tempted out by the few sunny days we have had. Temperatures haven't matched the sunshine, with our weather still coming from the north and west, but at least the combination of the wind and sun has gone some way to drying out the fields which have been soaked through for so long. On a visit to my butterfly-recording patch on 13 April, I was welcomed by the sight of a small tortoiseshell, a peacock and a comma—only one of each but it was a start. Later in the day I saw a member of the fourth family of our winter hibernating species, the brimstone, flying strongly and purposefully along a roadside hedge. This is a familiar sight in spring, when brimstones will wander over large areas looking for the sole feed plant of the year's offspring—the buckthorn. In our area this will be the alder buckthorn, which is an uncommon plant locally—I know of only three sites around the valley. Three days later I watched two of these bright yellow insects feeding on the nectar from a group of primroses which grew on the steep embankment of a stretch of ancient woodland. The brimstone is an important pollinator of wild primroses, and as each long tongue reached down the flower tube to find the nectar, so pollen would become attached and be carried to the next receptive plant. Although the sun has brought the butterflies out, the winds have been from the wrong direction to encourage much bird migration. Nevertheless, the urge to reach their breeding territories has seen the arrival of two willow-warblers and a blackcap on 15 April, and several wheatears on passage. No doubt the same urge led to the departure of the siskins who had wintered in the garden and were last seen at the nut baskets on 10 April.

J. M. THOMPSON *26 April 1994*

NORTHUMBERLAND: The travelling baker no longer comes whistling into our drive, basket on his arm. In a community like ours we shall not starve by his absence, but a human contact has been broken. Like the policeman, even the doctor is a remote figure nowadays. And now it seems one of the last bastions of our villages is being seriously threatened: the shopkeeper has stubbornly held his own despite fierce competition from supermarkets, but unless we "use it, we will lose it". Already our post office has been sucked into the cramped premises of the tiny general store but, if this closes, many locals will face hardship and expense, especially the elderly and the young mothers. Pensioners regard our local shopkeeper not just as their friend and link with local gossip but his shelves are their larder. Unable to plan ahead, daily I see them tread a measure over the green for "half a pound of lard and a small white". Sid is probably dishing out daily newspapers with one hand and helping a mother to claim her family allowance with the other, but he always has a cheery word for everyone. There are still folk who think in old currency and this kind of service, offered with tact and patience, is unique. Those of us who are mobile must support our shop with increased custom and remember that, while we could survive at present without it, one day we shall rely on it too. At least some of our household cash must be diverted into the villages if those hard-pressed small stores are to survive. Within this century hardship for many has diminished and some of the bonds which held communities together have been loosened; but when it comes to the crunch, no outside body is going to solve this problem. Before it is too late, we should foster anew the community spirit, that abiding pleasure of country life.

VERONICA HEATH *23 March 1984*

SOMERSET: After the spate of mechanised hedging and ditching that severely barbered the sides of our lanes during the autumn, there is now evidence at every outing of the manual craft of hedge-laying. One particular stimulus is a competition to find the best hedge in Somerset.

Any hedge that beats the one in our nearest lane will be a deserving winner. A farmer told me that hedge-laying was a job he hated. He always reached a point of frustration at which he was reduced to tying recalcitrant springy branches down with string. My potential winning hedge lies along 250 yards of the lane at an even height of thirty inches. Its extraordinary trimness is set off by the unkempt condition of the hedge on the opposite side, whose individual stems and branches straggle untidily in a generally vertical direction. In the new-laid

hedge, the main branches, or small trunks, of sycamore have been cut near their base (at a circumference of eleven or twelve inches). The cuts go half-way, or more, through the wood, which is then snapped over, laid horizontally, and threaded through the smaller branches. Every four or five yards, the hedge is pegged with a piece of the cut sycamore shaped like a fork. It is a remarkable piece of craftsmanship, and a living hedge for years to come. There is not a piece of string in sight. In time, the new verticals will have grown to size and the cycle will be renewed. Government encouragement of this sort of restoration, and sponsorship of the Somerset hedge competition by the County

Council and other bodies, are parts of the movement to recreate something of the familiar lines of the landscape as it was before intensive farming turned homely groups of fields into prairies. But despite this latest movement in the direction of conservation and traditional craft, one small farmer not far away is evidently led by his own reading of the economic signs to turn his fields into a golf centre; the rectangular brick-built clubhouse is nearly finished, and bunkers rather than hedges break up the view.

JOHN VALLINS *23 March 1993*

ACHVANERAN: There are very few days when there is no note to be written into my natural-history diary, whether it is the fact that a pair of pied wagtails have come back into the garden or the first frogs' spawn is found. The diary is also useful to see what has happened in previous years and it often gives an idea of what to expect on certain dates. On the evening of 25 March I looked at the same date for 1993 and noted that a pair of mandarin ducks had flown into the larger of the ponds in the paddock. Half an hour later I went upstairs and looked down into the paddock at the ponds and the Indian runner ducks splashing around with the khaki campbells, and in flew a pair of mandarin ducks. The same date as last year and within the same hour! The birds swam to the bank with the female leading and spent the next ten minutes or so constantly preening, with the male occasionally stopping to look around as if on guard. Whether it is the same pair that nested last year in a box designed for golden-eye is difficult to say. Last year a pair brought off some ducklings and in late summer I saw the adult female with four juveniles down on the river. It is a mystery where the mandarins have come from as repeated requests for information in newspapers and on local radio have drawn a blank. Originally they would have been escapees from collections of wildfowl but last year I looked at the two birds through a telescope and there were no rings, so they may well have been from a brood in the wild. The next morning the birds were in early but this time on the small pond and the female looked incongruous when she flew up on to a "tit"-type nest box in an alder tree. After a few minutes the birds flew off down the strath but they were back that evening and the first I saw of them was the male flying up into the alder that supports the golden-eye nest box. He sat about six feet above the box and looked down at the female who was by the edge of the larger pond. Hopefully this means they will use the box again this year.

RAY COLLIER *21 April 1994*

THE LAKE DISTRICT: Watching badgers (or, more truthfully, watching for badgers, because to know that badgers are in a sett is no guarantee of seeing them) is one of the most uncomfortable, time-consuming and sometimes fruitless occupations anyone could devise.

Last night's gnat bites emphasise this all too persistently. Why, then, do it? Well—it is rather like fishing or beekeeping: the rewards can outweigh all discomforts and disappointments. One needs luck, too, as well as experience, like meeting four young badgers by chance as I did on one of the few warm May evenings recently when the world, after sunset, seemed to be breathing and expanding with a life of its own. The voices of grasshopper warblers reeling in the sedges and a woodcock riding overhead almost distracted my attention from a flicker of movement behind strands of honeysuckle on a shelf of earth above me, and there they were, four little badgers as oblivious of me as I had been of them until a few seconds before—and so they remained for almost half an hour. This was obviously a very new world for them and, to judge from their small size and their innocence, it was astonishing that their mother had allowed them out at all. Their round baby bodies were almost pinkish-grey in colour, tailed by ridiculous stumps and topped by small black ears, white-edged, and already the shining black and white badger face-blazon. They stayed close to the

sett mouth, moving very gently, shoving a little at times but not, as yet, playing. One dug, experimentally, in the earth and dislodged a stone which bounced down, loud in the quietness, and this riveted all four with interest but none was afraid. Indeed, they were completely confident until a pair of late whooper swans flew in, barking sharply to one another and, in a flash, there were no badgers at all—nor have I seen them since.

ENID WILSON *16 May 1966*

CHESHIRE: 12 March was a lovely spring day of warm sunshine, and the gales which had been tearing at the countryside during the previous weeks had dropped to only a stiff breeze. On the Common, there were great masses of frog spawn in the pond, but we could not see any of the long strings of jelly which distinguish the spawn of toads, for they prefer deeper water for spawning than that which satisfies frogs. Indeed, as we were walking beside the lake, we came upon a pair of toads mating, the male upon his mate's back, clasping her closely with his legs, as she crawled laboriously towards the water. She had trouble with the wire fence but, when we had lifted the pair over it, she made good speed over the grass and disappeared into deep water, still with her mate clamped firmly to her back. The eleven mute swans which had arrived on the lake in mid-February were still in residence. Although they were still showing some of the brown of their juvenile plumage, eight of the ten cygnets were swimming in pairs and engaging in courtship display with their necks stretched up and their breasts pressed together. It was good to see that the solitary coot of February had attracted another, so perhaps they will begin to breed again on the lake as they did in past years. All the black-headed gulls, which had been visiting the lake in varying numbers throughout the autumn and winter, had left for their breeding grounds. In the garden, a bumble-bee was on the wing, a ladybird had crept out of the refuge where it had spent the winter, and a comma butterfly, also tempted out of hibernation, was fluttering low above the still flowerless herbaceous border. It was a small male and, on the next day, it was sunning itself on the lawn. A friend tells me of two small tortoiseshell butterflies, two queen wasps and several seven-spot ladybirds at Burnley in Lancashire, also on 12 March.

L. P. SAMUELS *20 March 1990*

WEARDALE, CO. DURHAM: The wind carved patterns in the snow that fell overnight, lifting it over walls and dumping it in rippled, undulating drifts that buried footpaths and filled ditches. Knife-edged drifts trailed from the leeward side of fence posts, tree trunks and clumps of rushes in pastures. We waded and slithered along tracks that were sometimes clear, sometimes thigh-deep. The sudden cold snap arrived just after the mild winds of mid-February had loosened bud scales and coaxed gorse into bloom. Under the snow the shiny, spear-pointed leaves of cuckoo pint had already broken through the soil and the first primrose and celandine flower buds were open. Catkins, which should have been shedding pollen, hung withered and brown. Between snow showers the sky was clear blue from horizon to horizon. Every tree, wall and fence stood out against dazzling white fields. Tracks were everywhere: a squirrel's footprints crossing a bridge over a stream, a fox along the edge of a plantation, a smaller mammal—perhaps a stoat—leaving an indistinct trail in the deep snow. One set of rabbit tracks stopped at a brown, snow-spattered mound in the middle of the path. As we approached it lumbered painfully under a gate and into a field: a rabbit, almost blind with myxomatosis, its head swollen and joints stiff. It shuffled a few yards, then hunched in the shelter of the wall. Two fields away we picked up a

movement on the edge of a copse. A roe deer buck broke cover, followed by two does, and galloped across the fields towards another group of trees. Soon a tractor passed us and we followed its wheeltracks and the dry, dusty, sweet smell of hay and straw in its trailer. The sheep could smell it too and we heard their bleating long before we caught up with the tractor again. We reached them, clustered round the yellow pool of hay, just as the next snow squall blotted out the sun and swept over us.

PHIL GATES *11 March 1993*

OXFORDSHIRE: Probably not one in one hundred of the day-long procession of visitors which streamed in and out of the Forest on Palm Sunday knew what it was all about—all that concerned them was that this was the one day in the year when they could walk unchallenged in this lovely remnant of the ancient Forest of Wychwood. But among the true heirs to this tradition (both a right and a rite)—the inhabitants of the nearby village—there are still a few veteran traditionalists to whom this day is simply "Spanish Liquor Sunday". These bring in bottles containing an already prepared solution of medicinal liquorice and strong peppermint sweets, eventually to be diluted with water from a special spring, and then drunk, some on the spot, the rest taken home to be shared with the family. Although unrecognisable in its dialect form "Ussell", the original name of the spring, "Worts Well", is evocative of Anglo-Saxon herb-lore, and no doubt connected with the still herbal emphasis of the occasion.

But traditions are not immutable, and even on my first acquaintance with this ritual (which must have been Palm Sunday 1911) most of the invading villagers passed by the traditional site to the more accessible and artificial Half-moon Well farther down the valley. Since then

progress has continued even farther afield to the Iron Well, a chalybeate spring. Although some of the sticklers for tradition acknowledge that "By rights, us 'ad ought to get the topping-up water from Ussell", they meekly follow the crowd, shepherded by keepers, to the false Mecca. But since this adds a further mile to the springtime walk, who can blame them?

W. D. CAMPBELL 22 March 1978

THE LAKE DISTRICT: It has seemed for some time now that there are fewer otters in this district. They are certainly infrequent in their usual haunts and some of their traditional breeding places are forsaken—a mill at Cockermouth, a hollow under a road near Grasmere, and rock-holts near the head of Derwentwater are all deserted. The mill is ruined, its lade gone, and the other two places are made untenable by people and traffic. However, the recent stopping of otter-hunting in the south and the fact that it goes on here made me wonder, again, if there really are fewer otters or have they—like some Lake District dwellers—simply withdrawn to quieter places. I have walked many river-bank and lake-shore miles recently in search of otter signs. What was I looking for—not only otters but their "seals" (paw marks) or "spraints" (droppings) on favourite rocks; the little green trackways otters leave on meadows between one turn of a river and the next. I saw no otters and no spraints but I found some seals and one green track, used for generations, is still in use. Last week I wandered, early one morning, down a muddy path to the river and there, below straggly hawthorns, was an otter—but it was dead. It was a fine young female, struck, it seemed, by traffic on the road above, for there was a mark on her side and bright blood oozed from her mouth on to the spring green. She lay there, totally limp, surprisingly long (almost a yard in length), her thick-based tail curved back. The black leathery webs of her paws were furled now, like chestnut buds, her coat dewed with moisture.

ENID WILSON *31 March 1969*

MACHYNLLETH: They used to call it the sweet mart to distinguish it from an evil-smelling beast called the foul mart. Today we call it the pine marten, while the foul mart has become the pole cat. Both belong to the cousinhood of the stoat and the weasel but are bigger and darker than either. Both used to be widespread in Britain but they were wiped out by gamekeepers in many areas and managed to survive only in the wilder places. Until early this century their fortunes were similar: they seemed to be about to join the bear, the wolf and the beaver on the list of extinct British mammals. But with the reduction in gamekeeping from 1914 onwards, the polecat steadily increased. It is now common in Wales and has spread to districts as far away as Warwickshire. Yet the pine marten has made no such recovery except locally in the Scottish Highlands, where it is reported to be doing well and has even been filmed visiting bird tables and coming into houses for food. Meanwhile for some unknown reason it remains a great rarity outside its restricted localities in Scotland and Ireland. In Wales, because it is secretive and mainly nocturnal, it remains by far the least known mammal. For many years Snowdonia has been accepted as its Welsh headquarters with occasional records of it in nearby localities. But recently its probably Welsh distribution has been hugely enlarged with the appearance of an article in the current newsletter of the Llannelli Naturalists, which is consistently an excellent and reliable publication. In it a pioneer survey by Ian Morgan brings forward evidence that there are martens, though they may be extremely few, in the counties of Cardigan, Radnor, Brecon and Carmarthen. Ever since I came to live in Wales nearly fifty years ago I have longed to see martens and have always kept an eye open for them in Snowdonia. But from now on it looks as if I ought to turn my steps south rather than north.

WILLIAM CONDRY *10 April 1993*

GLOUCESTERSHIRE: Throughout the Easter weekend a feeble black ewe lamb lay in a cat basket as we struggled with frequently replenished hot-water bottles and one nutritional strategy after another, to coax her back to viability. Picked up from the hedge bottom at three days old, she was clearly in trouble, rectal temperature stood at 96°F compared to the normal sheep temperature of 101.6°F and only a glucose injection lifted her from an immediate demise. We worked out the cause of her decline. The twins were out in a short but heavy shower. The mother licked one dry and it continued to thrive. Poor little Topsey must have got wet, cold, failed to feed and rapidly sank into the downward spiral. I remain unsure that we have yet won on this front but she is back with her mother and twin sister even though regular supplementary nutrition is still needed. It won't be for lack of trying if she doesn't make it. And on Easter Saturday we had to rush one ewe along to the veterinary hospital at Wootton-under-Edge for a Caesarean section, an expensive diversion at the best of times and all the worse for the fact that this ewe has needed this top-of-the-market treatment two years running. So, she has had more expensive private medical treatment than we will have in a lifetime. This time she did get a live lamb out of it but we cannot risk this again so September will, I fear, see her recycled through a tin of cat food. Easter Sunday dawned bright and clear. What horrors would the day bring? I hear you ask. We did not have to wait long to find out. The last of the ewe lambs to come to full term got stuck after struggling to give birth for an hour. We got her under cover to find that the head and back legs were coming out together—this is an anatomical impossibility. My wife did brilliantly. She managed to rotate the lamb, push the back legs back and produce a normal delivery position. A fairly enormous ram lamb survived this trauma, as did its mother, into whom I promptly stuck a syringe of penicillin.

COLIN LUCKHURST *16 April 1993*

AGDEN CLOUGH: Great cauliflowers of cloud reared in the sky as we went up by Grindle Barn to the russet moor. The ash trees below the barn have that silver sheen about their twigs now, precursor of green buds and cuckoo call. The trio of gritstone buildings were put here on their tiny shelf exactly 340 years ago, perched on this fearsome pasture grade almost overhanging, it seems, the cascade in Grindle Clough.

It's many long years since hay was stored here by the resident of High House, or calves fastened up for the winter. There are still, though, the remains of manure in Grindle Barn and a horse rake and mowing machine under the adjacent wind-bent sycamore. Quiet remnants of quieter times. Having crossed the watershed near White Tor, we tramped the heather moor down to the meanders and shale banks of Strines Dike and so came through the giant beech trees to Mortimer Road in Bradfield Dale. In the early afternoon we climbed above Agden Reservoir to the cruck barn of Bowsen, sleeping still below its girdling trees at the southern end of Agden Rocher. The sun continued to shine and, here among the twisted little oaks, the chill spring breeze had died. We climbed higher up the square-cut holds of Huddersfield White Rock which form Agden Rocher and sat on the crest, where all the wide world seemed visible. I lay back on the tussock grass, legs dangling over the Rocher's rim. High overhead as I gazed, the cauliflower clouds were piled like fairy castles in the blue; was it possible that I heard the Shearing piano? Maybe only skylarks far away.

ROGER A. REDFERN *11 April 1985*

CHESHIRE: In these inflationary times, when they are so very expensive, it is worth remembering that a number of excellent substitutes for cultivated vegetables and salad ingredients can be obtained at no cost but the trouble of collecting them. Chickweed, one of the commonest of garden weeds, is now making luxuriant and tender growth and is a succulent if rather flavourless addition to a mixed salad. In former times, in fact, it was hawked in the London streets as a salad vegetable. Like young nettles, chickweed, if properly cooked and served, is as good as early spinach in both flavour and food value. Young dandelion leaves are often used as a salad vegetable, but not so well known are the young leaves and tops of brooklime, an aquatic speedwell or veronica often found growing in association with watercress. The chopped leaves of ramsons, the wild garlic, are a good substitute for chives. In Tudor times dishes of the flower buds of gorse and broom appeared on the best dining-tables, to be eaten between courses for their appetite-provoking bitterness.

Although I have as yet heard of no further spring visitors beyond the always early sand martins, chiffchaffs and wheatears, by the time that this note appears I expect that we shall have welcomed at least the first willow-warblers and swallows.

L. P. SAMUELS *12 April 1977*

MACHYNLLETH: On 2 January a magnificent wave (such as comes only once in 100 years) severely damaged the railway along our estuary, so providing professional pessimists with a field day. For them this meant beyond all question the end of the railway. The line had long been threatened with closure, they argued, and now the authorities had been handed the perfect excuse for abandoning it for ever. Well, the pessimists were wrong. BR got the cash from somewhere (certainly not profits from this ailing branch line) and very soon teams of men and trainloads of ballast were on the scene. Great work was done and last week we celebrated because the trains are running again. No doubt different people have different reasons for being glad that the line is restored. Some, being traditionalists, like to see the trains going by as trains have done for over a century. Others are pleased because just once in a while they actually travel by rail. My own reason for rejoicing is because I love to see the railway banks in summer with their spread of colourful wild flowers, their special butterflies and moths and their populations of small mammals, birds and lizards. But if the line were closed, its banks would quickly be invaded by sheep, which would nibble them until they were as bare and dull as the pastures on either side. So I pray that our railway has a long life still before it.

WILLIAM CONDRY *24 April 1976*

A COUNTRY DIARY

CHESHIRE and DERBYSHIRE: By the Easter weekend many wild daffodil and lesser celandine flowers had appeared, and a few of the small white blooms of barren strawberry were open on a dry south-facing bank. We heard no chiffchaff but four lesser black-backed gulls, flying purposefully towards the north, were probably returning summer migrants. On the eastern hills patches of snow were still lying, in spite of the persistent rain, but the first meadow pipits had returned to their breeding grounds, and chaffinches were singing in the woods of the upper Goyt valley and skylarks over the hill pastures. In a broad shallow valley on the county border a short-eared owl was quartering low above the ground, almost invisible against the dead brown herbiage until it displayed its pale underwings. The short-eared owl used to breed in several parts of Cheshire during the previous century but it is now best known as a winter visitor to western Wirral and the Frodsham marshes. Since 1971, however, breeding has been suspected, but never proved, in both Wirral and the eastern hills, and in 1975 a nest containing a small chick and a probably infertile egg was found on a marshy area by the River Mersey. It is hoped that the chick was successfully reared but, to avoid the risk of disturbance, no watch was kept upon the nest.

L. P. SAMUELS *4 April 1978*

SUMMER

SUMMER

OXFORDSHIRE: Atmospheric conditions during the recent hot spell have been ideal for filling the garden air, in the cool of late evening and very early morning, with an exquisite blend of scents, for which the honeysuckle clump and the sweet-briar hedge are mainly responsible, but just detectably owing a certain spiciness to the old-fashioned dame's violet or sweet rocket. Such perfumed periods were only met with on a few occasions when the hawthorn was in full bloom, and indeed on no occasion this season was the scent of the May so strong as to be, as it can be, verging on the objectionable—for apart from the sweet element which attracts bees to its blooms, there is also present another component which appeals to flies and other insects with a liking for animal excretary products. But the hawthorn is once again providing the almost infallible synchronisation of the fading of its blossom with the emergence of young starlings, and since the latter, with their parents still attentive, find hawthorns almost as good as oaks as hosts to numerous moth larvae, the annual coincidence of the two events is made most obvious. Hawthorn has also been much in my thoughts for the last few days, for a neighbour has brought me some seedlings of a pyracantha which she grew from the berries and which puzzled her because two distinct forms have resulted—one with foliage exactly like the seed-parent, but the other having leaves very similar to those of hawthorn but somewhat more elongated. I can only surmise that pollination from one or other of our native hawthorns, growing within a stone's throw of the pyracantha, has produced a bigeneric hybrid.

W. D. CAMPBELL *11 June 1980*

KESWICK: Apple-blossom time makes me miss my bees. I sold them a month ago and with them seem to have gone sixteen happy years. Beekeepers do not remember the wet years when honey was scarce and the bees hard to maintain, or the thundery summer evenings when the bees' tempers were (to put it mildly) frayed. One does not dwell on the back-breaking task of extracting honey in a hot, embattled kitchen, with all windows and doors closed against a horde of bees outside who have smelt honey and determine to get in, or on the cold, blowy winter nights when—for no known reason—it seems imperative to go and see that all is well in the apiary. Twice in my beekeeping years I have done that and found hive roofs blown off, or hives tilted by a gale. One remembers, rather, the hum of a contented hive at evening when the nectar flow—apple, clover, heather or whatever it may be—is good and the scent of it lies even on the air outside the hive, and one recalls, too, many other beekeepers—living and dead—for I still maintain that good beekeepers are (like fishermen) a different sort of people—slow, very patient and often gentle, with a humour of their own. One old man, now gone, who had kept bees for almost eighty years, spoke of his bees always as people and when they were getting what most people would call really nasty would only allow that they were a "laal bit cottered". He taught me a lot about life, too, as well as bees: "You can't," he used to say, "go against nature, only with her." I have kept an empty hive and, if times get easier, maybe next year, I still may watch my own bees on my apple blossom.

ENID WILSON *3 June 1965*

OXFORDSHIRE: Change for the sake of change seems to be the order of the day and, having at long last got used to the fact that my old Berkshire Downs haunts—with stone curlews and Pasque-flowers and the floriferous White Horse Hill itself—had become part of Oxfordshire by a stroke of the bureaucratic pen, I assumed that my stock of address labels, based on Oxford with a postcode, would last me for the rest of my days. Our little town (established by a market charter granted by Henry III in 1256) has more than doubled its 1,500 population of my boyhood and now has worldwide commercial interests ranging from furniture manufacture to technological services. And, of course, the name of Oxford in the address pinpoints our location most prestigiously. But now the Post Office has decreed that henceforth our local post office should cease to exist as a sorting office and that this function and the postmen concerned, should be based on Chipping Norton, seven miles away. The powers that be have failed to realise that, apart from the prestige of Oxford in the address, the new postal centre is cut off nearly every year whenever snowdrifts block the roads (as they did last winter) and that our little town, unlike "Chippy", has a much-used mainline service to Paddington. Having got this grouse out of my system, I have received a letter from our only bank (Barclays) informing me that from September the nearest branch will be at Witney, seven miles away. To complete the general feeling that things are going from bad to worse, I have just heard that our popular Good Food shop, the source of decent bread and pies, is to close.

W. D. CAMPBELL *24 July 1991*

NORTHUMBERLAND: The aroma of smouldering oak chips hangs heavily over the cove of Craster and a queue of connoisseurs is forming outside the fish shop. It is kipper time. Only the choicest herring are brought for this delicacy, locally recognised as the miner's high tea. The fishwives were busy, hanging the fish on tenterhooks after they had been gutted and soaked in a tank of brine to cure. The smoking shed bustles with activity and a woman in a long rubber apron carries a cran of golden kippers into the shop. "I reek when I gan home," she said cheerfully. Even in midsummer the supply of fish is controlled by the weather and with generations of experience behind them fishermen on this coast take no chances. When the fleet brings in a shoal of "silver darlings" the yard will be at work twenty-four hours a day. Frozen fish are not suitable for kippering; they must be fresh or the oil content is destroyed and the fish shrivel up in the shed. The flesh of a good kipper should lift off cleanly without any bones adhering to it, and then you will know if it has been cooked correctly. Baked in the oven or grilled, never fried. The succulent taste of a Craster kipper is an annual treat and, according to the woman who served us, the kippers have health-giving properties too.

After a picnic in the shadow of Dunstanburgh Castle, with the tide out we walked the rock-strewn beach line, dodging sanderlings, rock-pipits, oystercatchers and a turnstone. Both kittiwake and fulmar frequent this stretch of the coast for breeding, but these oceanic species spend the rest of the year out at sea. The fulmar is not a gull but a tubenose or petrel. An intriguing pelagic bird which must be one of the world's natural gliding experts.

VERONICA HEATH *19 July 1991*

CROOK, CO. DURHAM: The first painted lady put in an appearance in the garden last week, gliding over the hedge and settling on a patch of stocks. The arrival of these butterflies from North Africa always seems something of a miracle, and this one was especially welcome as 1991 so far has been a dismal year for butterflies in my part of Durham. By July the Hesperis seed pods in my flowerbeds usually host large numbers of orange tip caterpillars but this year, after a cold wet spring, they have failed to breed. Not so the slugs, which have undergone something of a population explosion. Large black slugs, *Arion ater*, have grown fat in the compost heap and glide over the mouldering garden refuse in wet weather like lumps of shiny liquorice. But even these are dwarfed by the great grey slugs. My several piles of old clay flower-pots—not to use but because I like the look of stacks of old clay flower-pots—are favourite hiding places for these tiger-spotted molluscs. The great grey, a fungus feeder, presents little threat to treasured plants, and its mating ritual is something to behold. The hermaphrodite slugs climb into bushes and hang entwined from a mucus rope, slowly rotating in mid-air for hours

while they exchange sperm. It took many early-morning and late-evening vigils before I observed this amazing ritual in a gooseberry bush. Great greys are not the only climbing slugs and I often found *Arion ater* climbing through the slender, swaying flower stems of flax plants. They seem to find the dying petals particularly tasty. Banded hedge snails are also great tree climbers at night, ascending the walnut tree to browse on algae. The garden at night takes on a new dimension and some plants come into their own. A large patch of Nottingham catchfly, barely noticed during the day, shines in the half-light, with elegant reflexed petals and long protruding stigmas and stamens, ready to brush against visiting moths. But it is the scents that are most memorable: honeysuckle, clove-scented pinks and stocks, and wild roses.

PHIL GATES *25 July 1991*

WEST CORNWALL: It now gives me a sense of satisfaction to look at a map of the south-west peninsula and to reflect that on foot, over a five-day period, we covered the sixty-mile stretch from Newquay down the north coastal path to Sennen. At two points substantial rivers break the coastline—at the Gannel, just west of our starting point, we depended on the rowing-boat ferry—but at Hayle, superficially a much bigger obstacle, we benefited from careful timing. By arriving at the river-mouth at dead low water we were able to ford the bed of what is, at high water, a navigable channel for small coasters, and thus avoid a three-mile detour inland to cross the river and get back to the coastal path. It was only in close proximity to the coastal villages, especially the tourist resorts, that we met other walkers and overwhelmingly they were of the variety which regards the statutory quarter-mile from the parked car as a major excursion. Only once, on our final stretch from Pendeen to Sennen, did we meet another genuine long-distance coastal walker—identifiable by his high-pack rucksack. So for most of the long cliff stretches between settlements the path seemed little used and the extent of encroaching vegetation on some stretches suggested that a good patrol of walkers later this summer will do much to keep the track clearly evident. Vandals in this part of the country seem to exercise their skills on the pleasant wooden signs erected by the Countryside Commission, more of which appeared as partly wrecked than in their original condition. The long cliff stretches gave pleasant bird sightings and just below Nancekuke the amusing sight of a badger scuttling down a steep grassy bank to his sett. Above Aire Point a sparrowhawk rode the updraft from the cliffs and house martins flickered above our heads by the stone cottages at Cape Cornwall. The sun shone warmly over the last miles to Sennen, so we broke the walk for a swim in the translucent waters at Gwenyer beach.

COLIN LUCKHURST *22 July 1978*

MACHYNLLETH: Lately I have received reports of two rare creatures of the Welsh uplands which have always eluded me, one a mammal, the other a bird. The mammal is the pine marten. And no matter how uncommon it is I feel that, given just a bit of luck, I ought by now to have had at least a glimpse of one during a lifetime of walking the Welsh hills and forests. The marten is an animal able to live in rocky uplands but is probably happiest in woodland. And it was a marten hastening up through branches that a friend of mine saw a few weeks ago on the hills near Barmouth. Dark brown, bushy-tailed and twice as long as a squirrel, a wild marten must be a splendid sight anywhere any time. But it is so elusive and unknown that naturalists rarely go out to look for it deliberately. Things are different, however, with that rare bird the dotterel. This little plover has calling places which it visits on the spring and autumn migrations. The snag is that these brief halts along the route are often on the mountain summits and probably keep to no very regular timetable. Over the years I have

climbed to many a Welsh peak at what seemed likely dotterel dates but never had any success. So you can imagine how I feel when people who are not especially interested in dotterels casually report seeing them on the uplands. Recently I was shown a photograph of a dotterel taken on the Black Mountains by someone who didn't even know what it was. But I suppose the mountain gods have to have their little jokes.

WILLIAM CONDRY *18 July 1981*

CHESHIRE: The Black Lake in the centre of the common, which Alan Garner described as such a creepy place when *The Weirdstone of Brisingamen* was published twenty years ago, would scarcely be recognised by him now. The once slimy shore is covered with reed-grass amongst which a colony of its cultivated variety, striped ribbon-grass, is flourishing and the dark water is relieved by wide beds of reed-mace on which the bulrush heads are already well developed. Pond-skaters were sliding on the water in endless jerky motion. They look harmless enough but they are carniverous bugs and can dive to catch their prey if necessary. It was pleasant to see that the coot pair, for the third year in succession, have had a successful breeding season and were accompanied by three half-grown youngsters. Although the ling, the true heather, is still colourless, the cross-leaved heath is coming into pink flower. In the birchwood which surrounds the

common, a family party of jays were calling. The screech of young jays is a nostalgic sound for me and, whenever I heard it, I am back at school in summer terms long ago when evening prayers in the house-room were frequently enlivened by pet birds, which had been hand-reared, flying in through the open windows and making noisy, and often messy, circuits of the room. The spotted orchid is as common in Cheshire as it is in most of Britain, but I have seldom seen such a fine display of it as is growing on the old RAF camp at present. A wide area is covered with the pale purple blooms over which burnet moths and meadow brown butterflies were fluttering in the sunshine.

L. P. SAMUELS *28 July 1981*

PEEBLESSHIRE: Much domestic pleasure has recently been occasioned by the recognition that a family of hedgehogs have re-established themselves somewhere in our largely overgrown garden. We used to have a lot of hedgehogs in residence, and a splendid job they did in hoovering up the slug population. However, quite unwittingly, we drove them away when we introduced half a dozen free-range hens. From their old brick-built house in the vegetable paddock, the hens roamed all over the garden and their scratching and dust-bathing under the beech hedges clearly deprived the hedgehog population of safe refuge. I even suspected that the mounds of dead leaves and twigs they prepared for hibernation in the hedge bottoms were destroyed by the chickens and, as a result, for the past two summers we have never seen a hedgehog. So you can imagine our pleasure now at seeing both adult and infant hedgehogs on their evening perambulations. Saucers of milk have been gratefully accepted, and it looks as though a natural balance has been re-established. Only three of the flock of hens now survive—and after stray dogs and natural mortality have taken their toll, only humanitarian considerations prevent us slaughtering these survivors of a battery-unit infancy. They certainly do not earn their keep, for we are lucky to find a solitary egg on alternate days. So old are they in productive terms that one lays eggs which have soft shells and the third is altogether past it. Another absentee group, although its disappearance has nothing to do with the hens, has been the swifts, which used to appear at nests in the woodshed. The fault here is mine. Summer logging and the storage of timber for the wood stove have clearly made them feel less welcome.

COLIN LUCKHURST *11 July 1981*

MACHYNLLETH: Lately I have been trying a little bird-table experiment. One day I opened the french windows of my writing room and brought the tray of bird seed and the suet-and-nut cage indoors. It didn't take the bird-table regulars long to discover where their food had gone, and in a day or two there were bluetits, great tits, a robin, a chaffinch and several green finches feeding and fluttering round my room, perching on my lampshade, my books and my deckchairs as if these were things they'd been used to all their lives. But what I did not expect was the tameness of the woodpeckers, who soon became the boldest of the crowd. It was a strange experience to sit writing in my room with a woodpecker hammering at nuts at the other end of the table. Another of our garden regulars who longs to join the feast is a jay. But he cannot yet nerve himself to cross the threshold. Instead he perches on the terrace and looks in for several minutes. Then off he flies as if perplexed by the whole affair. What I have chiefly learned by my experiments is that all the stuff written about certain individuals being able to attract wild creatures because of some mystical affinity with them is so much sentimental twaddle. Anybody can be a St Francis among the birds. All you want is lots of lovely food to give them, preferably in a peaceful, tree-shaded garden with no cats.

WILLIAM CONDRY *4 July 1981*

NORTHUMBERLAND: A friend invited me to go driving with her in her pony trap. Having ridden all my life, it was interesting to compare disciplines. We bowled along at a steady trot for the whole hour. Had I been hacking, the horse would have demanded a change of pace, but a driving horse gets into rhythm and prefers to maintain the trot. When we called at two farmhouses for a drink and a chat, the pony switched off, standing relaxed and motionless as long as we wished. A riding horse would have fidgeted, wanting attention after a decent interval. It was a lovely way to see our countryside, the hedgerows and dry-stone walls tumbling down deep, bosomy hills. The pair of partridges on stubble, the foal stretched at ease in the long grass, coots and dabchicks on the reed-margined streams. We bowled over the old hump bridge, where I noticed stress cracks which moss and ferns were filling. One village of beetle-browed cottages was *en fête*, its ivy-covered inn decked out with a plastic banner. A good coachman can train herself to be a good judge of pace. Apparently, the way to acquire judgment is to watch the horse and see how long it takes him to go from milestone to milestone. About six minutes a mile is a fair pace: after a time, when a driver learns road sense, it becomes easy to judge pace. The secret of good driving is good—i.e. sensitive— hands. These are reputed to be a gift, but they can be improved by practice. It was a joy to be driven by someone so expert: perfect rhythm, the well-sprung dog cart moving in unison with a well-managed pony, every buckle adjusted to a nicety—maximum power with minimum strain. Two well-upholstered, middle-aged ladies in the trap must have been a fair weight to pull up our hills, but the little chestnut achieved it with aplomb. He was enjoying himself as much as we were.

VERONICA HEATH *17 August 1990*

THE BURREN, IRELAND: It is night. Darkness and wetness lie heavy on the Burren. A tall figure, raincoated, hooded, with bucket and trowel, stalks by flower, vegetable and herb beds, stooping now and then. It is Mary Ann, snail and slug hunting, and the Burren slugs are enormous. Her best tally is 222 gathered in forty minutes. I suggested drowning them in Guinness or Murphy's, letting them die happy, but she upends them. Yet, as I learned recently, slugs are not untouched by passion, nor is the world of gastropods wonderless. They are hermaphrodite but do not self-fertilise. Instead two courting slugs aim love arrows at each other. Mating lasts several hours with dual penetration. With Chaucer, we cannot say we "wol have no slogardie anyght" though "The sesoun priketh every gentil herte!" Snails, poor things, were used to cure warts. The warts were rubbed with a black snail, which was then impaled on a thorn tree. The warts withered with the snail, finally disappearing—a form of psychotherapy, implying the idea of wasting. We walked on the Rine with our dear American friends, Rita and Mary Ellen, and saw a sea otter, our very first sighting. It took full note of our presence, watching us each time it surfaced. We could see its flattened head and off-white chin and neck. In mid-July, I am pleased to report, the seals, frightened away in April by the activity around the grounded French factory ship, returned to the Rine. At the end of July we saw "our" pine marten

lolloping about in a circle on rocks surrounded by knapweed, bugle, harebells and few lingering spotted orchids and cranesbill. Another morning at 5.40 I watched a fox amble down our drive as if it owned the place, and so it did! It had a magnificent brush—may it keep it for ever and thank goodness the Clare Hunt is a Drag Hunt.

> "Now I adore my life . . .
> With the Fox, the questing Snail
> And the Eye altering all;
> And I dance with William Blake."
> (Apologies to Roethke.)

SARAH POYNTZ *15 August 1991*

JOHN RADCLIFFE HOSPITAL, OXFORD: I rose at 4.30 a.m. on 4 August, for two old friends (one a former pupil) had invited me to join them in a bird-ringing session in their reed-bed site by the Thames near Goring. After the mist cleared birds began to move and on a calm, sunny morning we caught and ringed about twenty-five birds, sedge- warblers predominating but with a sprinkling of others such as reed- and garden-warbler, blackcap, whitethroat, robin, bluetit and willow-warbler. Sedge-warblers are the target species here, and over the years much information has been accumulated concerning their journeys to winter quarters in Africa, and also data on age, annual returns to the same nesting-sites and the striking ability of this tiny bird to put on weight rapidly to fuel up for the Sahara crossing. Apart from the main object of the visit, the wetland flora, including abundant meadow-sweet (swarming with a small species of hover-fly) and sneezewort, and plentiful dragon-flies, provided further interest, but the highlight came just as I was about to leave around midday, for two young hobbies appeared and circled overhead, presumably in search of dragon-flies. On the way home late in the afternoon, the early rise, and the long spell in fresh air, began to tell, and at one point early on in the thirty-odd-mile journey I felt momentarily drowsy, but quickly pulled myself together. Then, within half a mile of my house, there was a terrific impact with a tree on the other side of the road, and that is why I am writing from the present address. The main damage is a fracture at the top of the breastbone and numerous gashes on forehead and wrist needing stitches. Apparently I am making satisfactory progress, and am now allowed to get up and walk a bit, and eat a little. I am in the short-stay ward, which sounds promising. The team of women who look after me are marvellous: bless them all, and, of course, the doctors and surgeons.

W. D. CAMPBELL *14 August 1991*

MELTON CONSTABLE, NORFOLK: The woodlands around this central Norfolk village are one of the remaining areas where it is possible to see spectacular carpets of wild bluebells. However, there are now two plantations just off the main road where the luxuriant spread of hyacinth-coloured flowers will not be back for many years, if ever again. Their absence is the work of an unscrupulous team who systematically stripped the woods of their bluebell bulbs earlier this spring. The bulbs then earn them substantial profits when resold to horticultural dealers. The flower extraction at Melton Constable is not an isolated incident: this year in both Norfolk and Essex protected species of orchid have been stolen from county trust reserves. The increasing public interest in growing native flowers in the garden has fuelled a nationwide demand for the seeds and bulbs of beautiful wild species. Bulb-lifting cowboys have seen the chance for a quick profit and moved in. Currently, clearing out bluebell woods is not illegal if the landowner gives consent. Though the bulb gangs are not too worried about legalities. The team that cleaned out Melton were arrested earlier this month for stealing snowdrop bulbs at another site in Norfolk. Whatever the current legal position, plundering the countryside of its wild flowers must be morally indefensible, making further inroads into an already diminished flora. Just two examples of this loss are the disappearance of ninety-seven per cent of traditional meadowlands since the 1930s and half of all British woodlands since 1945. Plantlife, an organisation recently established by a group of dynamic environmentalists, with David Bellamy as its president, is exclusively concerned with conserving the British flora. It is now campaigning to stop the kind of activities that took place at Melton. One way would be to encourage responsible landowners to outlaw the practice by withholding consent to the bulb gangs. Other possible measures might be for the horticultural trade itself to sell only seeds legitimately produced in cultivation, and for the public to buy only those that were labelled as such.

MARK COCKER *5 August 1991*

HAM RIVERLANDS: These riverlands lie in a loop of the Thames. They qualify as "waste ground", that term used in floras to cover so many riches. Now the grass is the colour of dry sand, giving a surround to the scrubby bushes and trees, mostly hawthorns with

berries turning to red. Brambles festoon themselves and already the fruit is juicy. More surprisingly, there is a pear tree as well as apples and plums dotted around. Hops and traveller's joy ramble over things with their delicate flowers. Yellow is the predominant colour. Bushes of vetch and trefoils, various hawkweeds, St John's wort, tansies, evening primroses and toadflax interspersed with rosebay willow-herb, knapweed and chicory. A very ragged group of ragwort was struggling against an invasion of cinnabar moth caterpillars. Ragwort is a certifiable agricultural weed because of an alkaloid poison in its leaves. If the leaves remain in grass cut for hay to feed cattle, the animals do not recognise it, eat it and the poison destroys their livers. The moths and caterpillars manage to store the poison in such a way that they are unharmed but any predator is affected. The caterpillars chewing up their poison were vigorously striped in yellow and black bands, making them look like a huge Rugby team. No doubt, the ragworts will recover. A greater danger comes from the marauding Japanese polygonum springing fully armed from the ground ready to obliterate anything in its path, like a concrete tower block erected on the village green. Whilst charting its advance we found a deserted badger hole. Careful scrutiny revealed a badger's hair and the skeleton of a fish. We walked on through the gathering dark and the swooping bats down to Teddington Lock, where the neat order of lock-keepers maintains grass and flowerbeds in impeccable order.

AUDREY INSCH *17 August 1987*

WEARDALE: After a week of incessant rain and thick mists, a clear, bright morning was too good to waste. We climbed from St John's Chapel up to Sedling Rake, a rough track along the northern flank of the dale. Some low-lying stretches were still quaking peatbog, squelching underfoot and threatening to engulf our boots. Earlier in the week the downpour had turned steep sections into a temporary river, washing away soil and leaving a path of sparkling, amethyst fluorspar. The lead-mine spoil tips all over the dale are full of this mineral and when they're used as hardcore for upland tracks the result is always the same: a jewelled footpath. By noon the warmth of the sun had dried out sodden thistle heads that attracted small flocks of linnets and goldfinches. Apart from the mountain pansies that will flower until the first frost, the thistles are the most colourful element in the autumnal flora of the high pastures. Each seed head is a microhabitat, containing tiny yellow fly larvae that probably supplement the goldfinches' vegetarian diet. There seems to be little invertebrate life in these rough grasslands but it is there, hidden in microhabitats: insects in seed heads, ground beetles and ants' nests under rocks, crane-fly larvae in moss tussocks. With the sky clouding over we took the sheltered route back, following the river Wear from its source at Wearhead, where the Burnhope and Killhope Burns unite. At the abandoned West Blackdene fluorspar mine, where the Wear squeezes between rock ledges and is narrow enough to jump over, a vigorous young tree caught my eye. It was an alder but with female flowers that were three times larger than the native species and with smooth, shiny pear-like leaves. It was an Italian alder, a tree more at home in Corsica than County Durham. How it managed to slip in amongst a planting of nondescript ash and sycamore saplings will probably remain a mystery, but it makes an exotic addition to the local flora.

PHIL GATES *23 September 1993*

KESWICK: There is a tendency for natives here to go to ground at the height of the season—if they can. I am no exception; walks are early or late and the garden gets the rest of the day. There is no lack of work in August and in doing it all sorts of things come to light which, else, might be overlooked. Raspberry picking showed a new buddleia seedling in the canes and cutting out the fruited blackcurrant wood let sun in to small blue-flowered borage plants and lemon balm whose scent is an anodyne on a sticky afternoon. What last year was a vegetable patch has been grassed over to become field again and in its new growth there is more borage as well as red poppies, clover and even caper spurge. All were unexpected but the greatest surprise is the flowering of a bamboo thicket which is over forty years old. It has never done it before. Bamboo is known to be a capricious, almost mysterious, flowerer and when plants in the south were blooming unusually well in the 1960s mine did nothing. The plant is really a tall grass and the flowers are grasslike—purplish-brown spikes with lemon-green stamens which tremble at the least breeze. It used to be said that they died after flowering but surely this is a myth. Mine, like a lot of things in this garden, seem to be in rude health, so I wonder if bamboos elsewhere are also in bloom in this strange damp year.

ENID WILSON *17 August 1981*

THE LAKE DISTRICT: When the cars are crawling bumper to bumper through Ambleside and the fells are "wick wi' fwoak" I sometimes go into the "back of Skiddaw" country to get away from it all. Here, even in the August holidays, you can be reasonably sure of having untracked hills to yourself and a mountain day free from the irritations of traffic, crowds, noise, litter and all the excesses of mass tourism. You could hardly call it exciting country—the only climbing crags are on Carrock Fell—but the spaciousness of these lonely, heather fells, the vast views stretching from the familiar peaks of central Lakeland to the Scottish hills, the welcome absence of tracks and cairns, and interesting, even dramatic, links with our distant past together provide an unusual flavour not found elsewhere in the national park. The ruins of the early British hill-fort more than 2,000 feet above sea level on the summit of Carrock Fell, for instance. Why was it built, and how? And the old derelict mines tucked away in remote gills, miles from anywhere; what incredibly hard lives these men must have had in these dark tunnels and shafts so high in the hills! There are nine summits of more than 2,000 feet in this desolate country that John Peel and his little Galloway knew so well and you can collect them all in a far from demanding day—except, perhaps, in bad weather, when you'll need to steer by compass. Knott (2,329 feet) is the highest, High Pike the most northerly summit in the district, and remote Great Sea Fell the most flamboyantly named. Not to be compared with the real Scafell, of course, but I have seen views, in shredding mist, from its rounded summit of a Mediterranean blue Solway and the sunlit Lowland hills that made one feel good just to be alive.

A. HARRY GRIFFIN *24 August 1981*

BOLSTERSTONE: Of all the hilltop villages in this part of the country, none sits more solidly upon its ridge than Bolsterstone. Up here the Pennine air seems always fresh because we are almost 1,000 feet above sea level. The other day we took the ridge-top path that runs eastwards from the village. There wasn't a breath of breeze under a cloudless sky. No sound came to us as we went along through wiry grass burnished by a rainless month and late harebells were still shining bravely. Cows were grazing the high pasture over the wall to our left as we sat to look back. The squat tower of the dark-stoned church crouched among its graveyard trees, but we could see nothing of the medieval castle that once dominated the settlement. Below our belvedere, to the south, More Hall and Broomhead reservoirs, like the harebells, reflected a Mediterranean sky. At the head of Ewden Dale, beyond the reservoirs, the purple profile of the Broomhead Moors dominated the horizon and, now and then, we heard the "pop, pop" of a shooting party on what was, in Edwardian times, England's record-breaking grouse moor. However, our immediate ridge-top world was quiet. Over the wall a resting cow had her eyes closed and ears back as she chewed her cud. An ear flicked off a visiting fly. We were all at peace up here. Further along the deep woods of Wharncliffe came into view, across the great space of the Don valley, and above the woods the brown pastures of Wharncliffe Chase—highest of stately parklands where once North American bison roamed. We had reached the ridge-end, at the crumpled top of Townend Common, where long-gone quarrying has left complex earthworks covered by desiccated moor grasses. It is a major viewpoint, looking out beyond Stocksbridge and Deepcar across the multi-hilltopped South Yorkshire terrain. We saw, too, the little eminence of Walders Low on the grassy ridge-top halfway back to Bolsterstone. Here lies an ancient chieftain who has left his name in other places locally; though dead these many centuries he would surely readily recognise this unchanging grassy ridge country.

ROGER A. REDFERN 21 September 1991

CROOK, CO. DURHAM: When I answered a knock at the door I found four of my daughter's schoolfriends holding a plastic box at arm's length. Inside was a fat, brown elephant hawk-moth caterpillar—the first I had seen since the species bred on the bogbean in my garden pond four years ago. When we released it from its temporary prison it obligingly went through its defence repertoire, first rearing up on its hind legs and swelling up at the front, so that the two pairs of false yellow and black "eyes" glowered at us, then snaking violently from side to side. The species gets its name from the first few segments of the larva when it is feeding, which look vaguely like a prehensile elephant's trunk. Early last summer was poor for butterflies and moths locally but by the beginning of this month the situation had improved drastically. Last weekend in Hamsterley Forest we counted over 200 peacocks on creeping thistles along about half a mile of woodland track. The most memorable butterfly spectacle in the garden involved the commonest of species, the cabbage white. This year I grew a sweet pea called White Southbourne, trained up wigwams of canes. It was while I was picking a bunch that a veritable flock of cabbage whites hove into sight. There were three females and eight males, and their wild, spiralling courtship chase took them between the sweet-pea wigwams, so close that I could hear the rustle of their wings. There were moments when it was difficult to distinguish between butterflies and flowers, before the insects split into three groups and went their separate ways. The whole butterfly ballet, with the insects blending with the flowers, had the surreal quality of Walt Disney's *Fantasia*. However, the eggs left behind on my broccoli were real enough; the leaves have been reduced to skeletons.

PHIL GATES *19 September 1991*

THE LAKE DISTRICT: Somebody has been out in the fells during the last year or so rebuilding summit cairns with something of a craftsman's skill and even, in some cases, the eye of an artist. The latest I have noticed is on the summit of Mardale Ill Bell—a solid, triangular piece of careful, dry-stone masonry topped by a rough wooden cross, not unlike the decoration on many Alpine peaks. High Street, Dale Head, High Spy and several other tops all have rebuilt cairns—some of them slender structures that may not withstand the winter ice and gales but must have involved a great deal of patience and skill. None of these new edifices is offensive; several are aesthetically pleasing, providing graceful foregrounds to a mountain picture, and this recent wave of neat building, using material readily to hand, is vastly to be preferred to the wholesale wrecking of handsome summit cairns carried out a few years ago. The fine cairns on Pike o'Blisco, Lingmell and Dale Head all suffered in this way, while the historic Robinson memorial cairn near the foot of Pillar Rock was regularly torn down. Our fells are disfigured by a ridiculous profusion of so-called route cairns—one-tenth the number would be more than ample—and most of them are far too big; unhealthy repositories for discarded sandwiches and apparently sited for tripping the feet in darkness or mist. Further, this surfeit of cairning often swamps the significance of the few really important ones. But tidy summit cairns harm nobody and can be important navigational aids.

A. HARRY GRIFFIN *12 September 1977*

THE BURREN, IRELAND: It was a relief to see the rain falling after weeks of near aridity with dust being flung on to the hedgerows and their wild flowers. To breathe was to feel the delicate freshness of the renewed air; to gaze was to notice the renaissance of the wild fuchsia which, so to speak, "palely loitered" during the heat. Now it is vivid with colour beside orange hawthorn hips, above flaming montbretia and in our own Burren garden, lavender. Soon we hope to make crab-apple jelly and blackberry jam. This may even be the year of the sloe gin! Four years ago we had some fruit trees planted, two of them being apple. Unfortunately they were sited in an unsheltered, open space with the result that only the apple trees bore fruit—*one* apple each year, always knocked before ripening by the birds. However, we were lucky this year. We watched this beautiful, perfectly round apple reddening. Then one morning at about six the fruit was gone. We rushed out before the birds could get too busy and there our apple lay on a nest of grass. We ate half each and it was delicious, just as I'd always imagined that original Eden apple to have been!

There was great excitement in the village of Ballyvaughan recently when news arrived that a grant of £8,000 had come through to help renovate the old school as a community centre. This, added to more than £17,000 collected by the Ladies' Club (the population is about 400), brings construction a great deal nearer. This is but one example of the kind of people who live in this landscape: decent, caring of the beauty they live in and so very anxious to preserve it. As Ibsen said, "A community is like a ship" in which the ladies were "prepared to take the helm."

SARAH POYNTZ *7 September 1990*

Autumn

AUTUMN

CHESHIRE: San Francisco was basking in record high temperatures when I left on my flight home. Some twelve hours later I arrived in Manchester to an England well into autumn. The first few days after my return were mild and there was enough warmth to entice a late hibernating comma butterfly into the garden, where it quickly settled to feed on overripe fruit on a neighbour's palm tree. A walk through the local National Trust woodland confirmed the season, with the only prominent flowers in view being those of the locally over-abundant Himalayan balsam, and these will disappear after the first severe frost. I had hoped to see the autumn crocus in flower but could find no trace of it. Having been away for a month, I had probably missed its short flowering period. This is an unusual plant, in the family Iridaceae, with its leaves appearing in spring, but these have withered away before the flowers appear in the autumn. Bird life in the woods was quiet, with only the occasional outburst from a disturbed wren, and the song of a robin establishing its winter territory. I was keen to check if any little grebes had arrived on a favoured stretch of the river—a few winter here every year and on quiet days they sometimes venture on to the millpond. There were no birds on the pond, but a close scrutiny of the nearby river beneath some overhanging willows revealed two little grebes now in their winter plumage, preening and looking well settled. Siskins are also winter visitors to the woodland here and can usually be found in the Alder Carr. I could hear their call notes but caught only fleeting glimpses of the birds as they fed high up in the alders, their plumage blends in so well with the still green foliage. Recently, cold fronts have been moving down from the north, resulting in my first sightings of the year of redwings and fieldfares, although I have yet to see any flocks feeding on the well-laden local hawthorns.

J. M. THOMPSON *27 October 1992*

NORTHUMBERLAND: From the saddle we can see the fields bleached and shaven. The hedges are lined with skeletal heads of dried cow parsley and dockens, the grass is white with dew in the early mornings. Already there are signs of change, mottled trees and spent undergrowth in the hedgerows. Hawthorn and elder have tiny berries set and thistles are turning to fluff. I enjoy, from my elevated seat on the horse's back, the delicious sickly smell of the wild honeysuckle. Riding horses is a growth leisure industry and I have been helping a friend, who is North regional chairman of the British Horse Society, for some years, with her campaign to keep bridleways open. Last week a 100-mile riding route was officially opened. The Border County Ride is a direct result of my friend's and her helpers' liaison work. The ride is a joint project between the British Horse Society, the Forestry Commission's Forest Enterprise, Northumberland National Parks and the Otterburn training area of the Ministry of Defence. Months of work have gone into devising and researching the route, improving tracks and bridlepaths and signposting with waymarkers. The route goes from Kielder Water south to Bellingham, then heads north-east to Alwinton and our rugged border hills. After briefly joining the Pennine Way, riders just set hoof in Scotland before turning south to Falstone and back to Kielder. A horseman with a reasonably fit horse could ride the circuit in six days. Some of the bridleways have been little used but the terrain is not difficult, although there are minor hazards to negotiate like ditches, occasional stony tracks and fords over streams. Suburban horses do not like running water so the horse must be accustomed to getting his feet wet. Information on the Border County Ride is available from Forest Enterprises, Eals Burn, Bellingham, Hexham NE46 2AJ and gives a route description, maps, local shops, telephones, bed and breakfast for riders and horses, vets, doctors and farriers.

VERONICA HEATH *10 September 1993*

A COUNTRY DIARY

CLEY-NEXT-THE-SEA, NORFOLK: As we headed northwards, the car cut a wake through pools that were road-wide and six inches deep in places. Only hours after the autumn's severest downpour, great slabs of dark cloud cruised towards us overhead and threatened further rain. It was not an auspicious start to the day. Fortunately it proved to be a false omen. The storm had all but finished by the time we reached the coast. Yet, the gale-force winds elsewhere, in the Atlantic and North Sea, had set in train a substantial southerly movement of seabirds, and this had not slackened with the winds. Our arrival at Cley coincided with its peak passage off Norfolk. Two species—gannet and kittiwake—predominated. Gannets are powerfully built creatures, three-quarters of their world population nesting on Scottish sea cliffs. In adult plumage they are dramatic white birds with black wing-tips. However, almost all the gannets passing Cley were this year's brood and a uniform smoky grey. Kittiwakes, the most ocean-going of Britain's six breeding gulls, moved in even larger numbers, heading south for their winter quarters in mid-Atlantic. Among the constant stream of these two species was a range of more unusual birds: puffins, red-throated divers, manx and sooty shearwaters, great arctic and pomarine skuas. Of all forms of birdwatching, I think sea-watching is perhaps the most exciting, and also the most challenging. Many of the species mentioned earlier, especially the skuas, are separable only by relatively minor differences in size or shape. And with birds in flight, usually at considerable range and moving at some speed, there is no second chance of identification. Not only that; if there is sufficient swell everything disappears intermittently behind the troughs. It has also occurred to me that, of all forms of birdwatching, the sea-watch must appear the most bizarre to the lay-person. Seeing dozens, sometimes hundreds of figures huddled against the wind, eyes streaming with tears as they fix their binoculars or telescopes on what must look like an utterly featureless grey horizon, what does the non-birdwatcher make of it all?

MARK COCKER *14 October 1991*

CHESHIRE: By mid-September the colours of autumn were beginning to spread through the countryside. The long avenue of horse chestnuts was almost as much yellow and brown as it was green and the cherry tree outside my study window had turned gloriously scarlet, although the leaves on its extreme northern side were still green. Every autumn it is fascinating to see the colour creeping through the leaf-canopy from south to north. The chestnut trees, both horse and sweet, are thickly hung with the green prickly fruits which enclose the precious nuts. Neither is native to Britain, nor are they related to each other. The horse chestnut belongs to a botanical order (*Sapinadaceae*) of which there is no native representative in Britain. It was introduced during the seventeenth century from south-eastern

Europe and Asia Minor. The sweet or Spanish chestnut has been with us for much longer, having been introduced, probably, by the Romans. It is one of a large family which includes all our well-known catkin-bearing trees.

I was most interested in a recent Country Diary from Norfolk about the exhibition of bird art which I should like to have seen. I was, however, surprised that no mention was made of Archibald Thorburn, whose paintings of birds in their natural habitats surely have no equal.

L. P. SAMUELS *26 September 1989*

THE BURREN, IRELAND: I see two herons, each perched on a large rock above the ocean's surface, and between them, on lower rocks, seals and cormorants, some of the latter with wings outstretched. Overhead eight geese in V-formation wing for the open sea.

AUTUMN

Later another six follow. Light spreads, strengthens into full morning; colours change—slashes of flame, pale lime turn to red; slowly clouds cluster, accumulate until the waters shift into soft grey and silver with the hills green and light mauve. Not all the dawns of the past summer have been so fine or indeed visible. I remember once writing that even on wet days there is a clearing when a walk is possible. This summer proved me wrong and well I remember standing looking out at the Bay and thinking, if I were a stranger I would not even know it was there, so impenetrable was the draping mist, so omnipresent the sheeting rain. How glad I was then of our paintings by the Cornish artist Mary Martin and the Irish artist Manus Walsh. I could see again the loveliness of the Tamar valley—sunlit grasses, bluebells in Cotehele Woods, hill villages in Provence created by Mary. Invisible outside, the *Burren in Moonlight, in Spring*, painted by Manus, delighted us (his Chilean paintings too). We look at a landscape and rejoice in it. Good artists like these, combining in their creative insight integrity, truth and beauty, let us share their vision. We end, by sight and imagination, with several versions of the same landscape: our original view, the artist's embodiment of it and, coloured, framed by this, the prospect observed again. So enriched we return to the paintings to have life re-enhanced, saying with Monet, " . . . to him who lived there, this room would have offered the refuge of a peaceable meditation . . ." Rain sluices down. I am startled to see a bird, only the head visible, staring at me from the window-top—a wagtail, feet grasping the ledge-top, picking off snails, small, pink-shelled, whorls silver-edged. These will not "come and join the dance"!

SARAH POYNTZ *3 October 1991*

CHESHIRE: In the garden the ground under the tall birch tree and a large area around it are covered with the scales (or bracts) of the catkins and the so-called seeds, which are really minute nuts encased in a thin winged shell, which makes them very attractive to finches, and they are the only natural food that occasionally brings siskins into the garden. By chance, a few days before I had noticed the "seed" fall from the birch tree, I had listened to the shrill clear call-notes of siskins emanating from my neighbour's garden, and about a dozen of the tiny greenish-yellow birds flew from the trees and across my own garden without settling. The birch is the most beautiful of all the trees in Britain. Coleridge called it "The Lady of the Woods". It is ubiquitous in this country. It can stand extreme cold and dry situations, but not, apparently, great heat. It thrives in damp peaty conditions. Abroad it ranges from Scandinavia and northern Russia and southwards to the Mediterranean and Asia Minor.

A visit to the Common on 4 October was disappointing, for we had hoped the first mute swans of the autumn would have arrived. However, the only birds that we could see on the lake were a few mallard and many black-headed gulls, a single coot and the resident pair of Canada geese. Last year there were 7 swans on the lake on 22 September, and by mid-January they had increased to a maximum of 19. In 1990 there were 5 in September, and the herd gradually grew to 22 in mid-January 1991. The September News Letter of the Leigh Ornithological Society is as usual interesting. A charm of 60 goldfinches must have been a lovely sight, and a concentration of 86 great crested grebes on one of the flashes is larger than I have ever seen on a Cheshire mere. It was pleasant to read of sightings of the welcome alien the ring-necked parakeet.

L. P. SAMUELS *13 October 1992*

L. P. Samuels, a Country Diarist for more than thirty years, died late last Friday aged eighty-three, shortly after completing this diary.

NORTH DERBYSHIRE: Farming at the edge of a wood has its advantages: plenty of shelter from the elements, fuel, the close glories of spring and autumn. One of the prices to be paid, though, came to mind the other day when going up through the great wood from the Bull Field. I met a portly Friesian driven by her perspiring owner making good speed back to the pasture she'd escaped from. It reminded me of the day forty years ago when this farmer's father had called at the farm high on the hill beyond the wood. He looked at a Large White gilt and her four-day-old litter of ten. "I'll buy them off yer," he offered. The deal was done. How was he going to get the new purchases home? "I'll drive her and the little uns will follow on," he

predicted confidently. It was a hot afternoon and there was thunder in the air; the little caravan had barely left the yard when loud peals echoed from piled clouds. Heavy rain started to fall as a small lad ran from the field, asking if he could have a sack. "The farmer says he needs it for two of the piglets 'cos they'll not make the journey under their own steam," the lad explained. It was no surprise to the vendor because two of the litter were very small. The journey apparently continued through the wood in drenching rain, lit by lightning. With two piglets in the sack the farmer did his best to drive the gilt in the right direction, but the remaining offspring seemed to lack the sense to follow their mother. After a long, circuitous course involving some of the remoter corners of the great wood the contingent gained sanctuary at the wood-edge farm. The pair of bagged-up piglets joined their heartier brethren and mother in new quarters, put on weight and never looked back. They could have found plenty of free sustenance under the oak trees in the wood that autumn, but the farmer never risked another sortie of that kind!

ROGER REDFERN *16 October 1993*

THE LAKE DISTRICT: It was the first time my son-in-law from Vancouver had climbed a hill, anywhere. Hundreds of days skiing down them, in two continents, after ascents by chair-lift or cable-car, but no pedestrianism. So, on a bright but breezy day, all the Langdale Pikes were collected and a few scrambles thrown in for fun. My daughter, who used to climb, accompanied us and entered into the conspiracy so that Tony is still under the impression that our ascent of Jack's Rake and descent of part of the Dungeon Ghyll ravine are the easiest tourist ways. Once or twice, hauling himself up on greasy handholds or lowering a boot through the spray, he would mildly inquire whether this really was walking but we maliciously assured him that it was and he seemed satisfied. Perhaps he secretly sighed for the mechanical uplift of Mount Whistler, but surprisingly, his balance and footwork were impeccable—despite his huge, heavy Canadian boots being worn for the very first time. (I was wearing my magic "carpet slippers", which I now realise have their limitations.) The day, including the ritual real-ale session that rounded it off, was hugely enjoyed by all, although the youngsters seemed unused to the chill breeze on the summits. But two days later, on a round of the Gables, driving rain, battering winds that almost blew us off our feet and the usual mist put things in a different perspective. I had promised easy summit wandering and matchless views but the going, on a vile day, proved hard and we saw nothing. On the drive home, though, under the skirts of Skiddaw and Blencathra and along the Ullswater shore, the clouds were blown away and sunlit fells beneath a sky of deepest blue at least gave the visitors a sight of Lakeland at her best.

A. HARRY GRIFFIN *17 October 1983*

CHESHIRE: The thick riparian border of Himalayan balsam was fading, so that the creamy-white flower tassels of a colony of Japanese knotweed was particularly welcome. A pair of grey wagtails flew upstream. Presumably, like many of their species, they had deserted their traditional breeding territory beside the swift, rocky streams of the eastern hill country to nest beside our slow-flowing river. The prime object of our walk along this stretch of the river was to see whether one of our local rarities, the autumn crocus, had come into flower. It has not usually appeared before the last days of September, but so many plants have bloomed early this year that we thought the crocus might also have done so. However, we could find no sign of it, and the place where it grew has become overgrown with brambles and heavily trampled by blackberry pickers. In the long grass close to the river bank the crocus was always easy to overlook. A middle-sized tree was so smothered in wild hop, which had grown right to its summit, that we had to part its dense, rough foliage to see that its host tree was a hawthorn. It was thickly covered with the green cones of the female flowers, for the hop is dioecious and the inconspicuous male flowers grow on a separate plant. Mention of hops makes one think of beer, but when it was first introduced from the continent as a flavouring in the fourteenth century it met with considerable opposition. A petition to Parliament for its suppression stated that "this wicked weed would spoil the drink and endanger the lives of people". It was not until two centuries later that hops finally ousted the previous flavourings of marjoram, yarrow, sage and other herbs.

L. P. SAMUELS *19 September 1989*

GREENWICH PARK: One of the farthest outcrops of the North Downs, Greenwich Park gives startling views into the river valley beyond. Approaching the escarpment from the south is the Bower Avenue of sweet chestnut trees, some of them planted in the seventeenth century. In this country the fruit rarely matches our expectations, although the warm summer has ripened some very plump nuts. Visually the old trees are remarkable for their huge trunks heavily scored with a spiralling pattern. Queen Elizabeth's oak is reputed to have been planted at the end of the twelfth century. Last century it died and is now propped up, providing a satisfactory stand for a rampant ivy. On the flowering stems the leaves change their usual ivy shape and develop without lobes, often replacing them with wavy edges. The tomentose flowers with their globular heads present five heavily scented greenish-yellow petals to swarms of excited insects— wild and hive bees, wasps—all eager to gather the sweet nectar. Another autumnal pleasure at Greenwich is to stand on the meridian line of man's measurement and observe flocks of migrants high above with their own inbuilt navigational devices. The diurnal migration of the starlings, however, is more easily observed as they come back to the city to roost. At this time of year the home teams are augmented by continental immigrants, mainly from northern Europe. With high-pitched chatter they spiral down to chosen trees, maintaining a noisy presence for varying lengths of time until they quite suddenly all fall silent before rising in a boisterous cloud to continue on their way, or to circle high above the branches before hurtling down again to pick up their wild chorale. Lesser trees can be damaged, but at Greenwich they survive this high-winged treatment.

AUDREY INSCH *15 October 1983*

AUTUMN

KESWICK: Two days together last week were fit for gardening, an unexpected gift at this time of the year and one not to miss after so wet an autumn. There is always a strange feeling of leisure, of being suspended in time, in a November garden when the donkey work is mostly done, the vegetable patch dug over, the apples picked and stored, and the fruit trees and shrubs just biding their time until next spring. The soil is not yet too cold to plant and transplant and there is time to contemplate and decide where things could go to best advantage. So a special place has been made below a sheltering holly and thorn hedge for a new Cardinal Richelieu rose to replace one which died two years ago. This old Gallica rose is a smoky amethyst-red, so it has been put near a pale Maiden's Blush rose with newly rooted lavender cuttings behind a thick edging of silvery lamb's lugs. They are now part of a long border in front of the hedge, beyond which stretches the valley, the lake and the backdrop of the fells, which change daily and hourly with the sun or rain. Today is different, with a cold rain and a northerly wind stripping the last leaves from the birches. At noon, the garden seemed unusually still and silent; nothing stirred but the wind, and small wonder, for a sparrowhawk scythed round the house and through the bare apple trees to alight silently and gently on the top bar of the long wooden gate where raindrops hung. It crouched low, gazing intently along the hedges—a reminder (if one was needed) of the harder, hungrier months to come.

ENID WILSON *23 November 1981*

A COUNTRY DIARY

NORTHAMPTONSHIRE: It was a warm, sunny day for a cruise downstream on the river Nene from Oundle to Ashton lock. Two pairs of great crested grebes were swimming in the yacht basin and we were told that both pairs had bred successfully there earlier in the year. The waterfowl on the river were mostly predictable and included numerous mallard, occasional coot and moorhens, a few black-headed gulls and two pairs of mute swans with cygnets at widely separated points. A gaggle of fifty to sixty Canada geese was interesting for, in previous cruises at this time of year, we had seen only odd pairs. No cruise seems quite complete without a kingfisher, so we were delighted to see one fly rapidly upstream below a line of riverside willows. Big aeshna dragonflies zoomed low above the water but we saw no swallows or martins. Over a patch of seeding thistles, a charm of goldfinches was dancing. We moored beside a wooded island and had a picnic on the grass while a swan sat sunbathing on the cement surround of the lock, then we walked to the lovely village of Ashton. Abundant on a grey stone wall was pellitory, that curious aberrant stingless nettle with red stems and tiny green flowers. A mass of ivy covered much of the wall's top and two red admiral butterflies were feasting on the flowers. We bought drinks at the Chequered Skipper Inn and enjoyed them at a table on the village green. The inn displays a fascinating signboard showing, on one side, the upper side of the butterfly and, on the other, the underside, picked out in nails driven into the wood close together, their heads painted to make two excellent portraits of the butterfly. The chequered skipper is a scarce butterfly in Britain, being confined to a few restricted areas, of which one is the neighbouring Rockingham Forest.

L. P. SAMUELS *10 October 1989*

BRAEMAR: The roar of the stag now echoes in the remotest glens for this is the season of the rut. The throaty calls sound across the crags from unseen herds, while golden eagles spiral in the chilly autumn skies. On a recent day of broken cloud and slanting sunbeams, we went up the old, rutted track beyond Invercauld and came out of the pine woods close beside the foaming river. Here it comes bounding down from the black, shattered ravine called the Gullet with its border of pretty meadows punctuated by ancient silver birches. Slugain Lodge is ruined now, occupying strategic position where the valley narrows just before opening out to reveal the secret upper glen of the Quoich Water. Stalking parties from Invercauld would gather here long ago, on the way up or down the Quoich. We turned up the glen and contoured above the river, aiming for the big granite boulder—the Stone of the Priest—two miles ahead: an unmistakable feature on the route to the Sneck (the Notch), which separates Beinn a'Bhuird (3,924

feet) and Ben Avon (3,843 feet). From the Stone of the Priest there is a dramatic view to the west, up into the great crag-girt triple corries of Beinn a'Bhuird. They lie in deep shade on the sunniest day and, perched on the bulging wall of Bloodhound Buttress, above one of the highest lochans in the Cairngorms, it is easy to imagine you are the very last human inhabitant on earth. We had covered nine miles on gaining the windy watershed at the Sneck, and ascended 2,100 feet. Here at 3,100 feet above sea level we looked down into the head of Garbh Choire, where the impressive Mitre Ridge rears like an arete on Mont Blanc's Brenva face. The first dusting of snow highlighted its higher profile, portent of what winter must soon bring. A stag called from far down the northern glen as mist blew across Ben Avon's broad top, making our search for its huge summit tor an exercise in navigation.

ROGER A. REDFERN *28 October 1983*

CHESHIRE: The honey toadstool is one of the commonest British fungi and one of the most destructive to trees, its black rhizomorpha spreading upwards for a considerable height between the bark and the trunk, attacking the wood-cells, rendering their walls brittle and ultimately killing the tree. It was, therefore, with some perturbation that, on returning from holiday, we found a colony of huge honey toadstools clustered around the base of the big pear tree. The toadstool is usually comparatively small but these were eight inches across their caps, by far the largest that I have ever seen. We have, of course, removed the fungi but we fear that the damage has already been done. However, we console ourselves with the thought that we seldom get any eatable pears from the tree, for they are almost all shared amongst the carrion crows, starlings and wasps.

The honey toadstool is highly praised by some authorities for its edible properties, although I confess that I have never tried it. There is, however, another toadstool which is locally abundant at present which I have often mentioned in these notes and of which I cannot speak too highly as an esculent. This is the whitish scaly-capped lawyer's wig or shaggy cap, of which the young specimens are amongst the most delicious of all the fungi. Its texture is very tender, however, and it requires only the gentlest of cookings.

L. P. SAMUELS *4 October 1977*

CROOK, CO. DURHAM: Ever since this newspaper carried a story about a giant Chinese slime mould, I have received a steady stream of telephone calls inquiring about similar strange fungi. The reports coincided with the peak season locally for *Mucilago crustacea*—possibly the most common and certainly the most conspicuous British slime mould, but still minuscule compared with the Chinese behemoth. It looks like white, foamy custard spilled on the grass, where it creeps along engulfing bacteria and other choice micro-morsels. People finding this strange organism seem to fall into two categories: those who assume that it's something unpleasant and are thankful not to have trodden in it, and those whose curiosity gets the better of them. One of the latter brought me a *Mucilago* in her lunch box, excavated intact on a small square of turf. This was a well-fed example in the final stages of development and after sitting immobile on my desk overnight it began to change colour. By the middle of the following afternoon it had entered its reproductive phase, transforming into

small chestnut spheres of spores, like a mass of caviar in the grass. I have transplanted it into the lawn. The spores germinate into tiny amoeboid cells that wander around feeding, before aggregating into their "creeping custard" alter ego. I will be watching closely for its reappearance next autumn. This has been a wonderful season for other fungi in the north-east and telephoned reports have included a "chicken of the woods". Identifying fungi from telephone descriptions is a risky business, but this species is unmistakable. It is an almost fluorescent lemon yellow, tiered bracket fungus that sprouts from old tree stumps. It's edible, but is also long-lived and old specimens harbour other fungi that produce stomach upsets. Edibility ratings for toadstools in field guides apply to fresh, young specimens—a caveat that isn't always made clear. Experimenting with cooking older edible fungi can be a gastric trip into the unknown.

PHIL GATES *22 October 1992*

NORTHUMBERLAND: Mention of show leeks in my last Country Diary spawned a rash of green and white giants on our doorstep. Winter soups need leeks and the freezer means that I can get ahead with winter entertaining plans. The Romans introduced the leek to the North-East where large garrisons of soldiers were glad of its sustenance in harsh winter conditions; the leeks provided vitamin C, which prevented scurvy. A Geordie fever began, attacking men mainly but a few women are also victims and it knows no social boundaries. Doctors, teachers, butchers, the unemployed and the retired succumb to *Allium porrum "exhibitionii"*, which means growing leeks to exhibition standards. The gigantic leeks mature to reach the show bench from a late December or early January start. Cared for by a connoisseur they will increase their weight over nine months by nine million times, a feat only exceeded by the human foetus. The exhibitor must provide warmth, water, fertilisers, fungicides and pesticides in varying amounts and at critical times in a protected environment. One of my leek-growing friends says it is worth while because every entrant receives a prize corresponding to his position in the club show. "Last week I won a lawn mower," he told me. "If you don't want your prize you can take a voucher instead. You can't lose." During the months leading up to a show, money-raising events are held in order to swell the purse. These are held in a pub or working-men's club supporting the social importance that the leek still holds in this region. Although leek-growing success can come from a chance seedling showing size and quality, whose progeny will emulate it, more often it is a process of years of reselection to obtain the exhibitors' desired qualities. The champs must be edible; no hard woody centres run to seed are permitted. Jealousy can lead to theft and vandalism, even overnight decapitation, wiping out years of development. Dedicated exhibitors rarely take a holiday prior to the leek show.

VERONICA HEATH *8 October 1993*

AYLSHAM, NORFOLK: The livestock market held just outside the centre of this beautiful Georgian town every Monday morning is one of the great rituals of mid-Norfolk. Anyone living or even visiting the county should see it at least once; though go early—the place rapidly becomes crowded. Many of the rural communities surrounding you are of a vintage Thomas Hardy would have recognised and cherished, and some faces have the rich, comfortable character and idiosyncratic lines of an old oak settle. Yet don't be deceived by the rustic appearance: the leather patches on elbows, the subdued tones of the check, the tear, perhaps, at the jacket's shoulder, the unfashionable cut of lapel or trousers. Beneath that arched eyebrow is a shrewd instrument for judging life and its affairs. A fascinating portion of the market is the sale of household goods. Long before the auctioneer and his excited throng have moved systematically down the rows of lots, the prospective purchasers have examined and valued them. One of these lots can consist of an extraordinary mix: a disembowelled lawn mower, a second-hand chainsaw, coils of barbed wire, a box of yellowed 1950s paperbacks and a beautiful easy-chair that might go for scores of pounds down the King's Road. Here, in the heated moments of the bidding, its price might leap upwards in units of fifty pence and end after six forefingers have been raised momentarily. If Aylsham market is an expression of an older England, the café, standing in the middle of the grounds, suggests a forgotten age. At this time of the year the place is always busy, the windows steamed over and the interior thick with tobacco smoke. The bread is always white, the cakes home-made and the tea strong, hot and at a price that would give any Little Chef manager a bout of palpitations.

MARK COCKER *11 November 1991*

RICHMOND PARK: Many people assume that deer are daylight beasts like ourselves. Last month in the rutting season the stags' nocturnal roaring reminded us that darkness is their preferred time, even if they did stage some interesting antler clashes by day. Now calm has returned. Matriarchal hind groups graze together with stags moving in and out but showing no special concern for their own harems. Some of them are already tending towards the male club atmosphere, sitting together ruminating, with their eyes fixed on distant speculation. But whatever they do, stags inevitably catch the eye because of their antlers, the magnificent bone growth they have evolved. The Victorians proudly displayed those trophies but the early Celts saw deer as supernatural animals of the fairy world, capable of conferring both fertility and virility. The stag they saw as a fighter for good, trampling under foot the chthonic serpent of evil. However, we caught them in one of early November's brilliant quiet days. Mist rose slowly from the grass and evaporated through the dark-trunked trees, radiant with leaves of green, yellow, orange, gold, red and brown. Sound soared through the air: the harsh cries of the crows, the clear, sharp call of wrens flitting in the bracken and the querulous click of coots busy on the ponds. The fallow deer walked about with the strange stiffness they have if they are not trotting or running. Young does bounced about as if auditioning for *Bambi*. Two bucks lay on the grass unmoving while a group of starlings and jackdaws pecked around. One jackdaw found the choicest morsels on the deer itself and hopped up and down with excited pecks. As befits a noble animal, the deer paid no attention.

AUDREY INSCH *12 November 1983*

CHESHIRE: The National Trust's restoration of the mill-pool above the weir has now been completed and there is a sizeable lake. It is surrounded by the soil which accumulated during the excavation, and already this is almost covered with vegetation. Conspicuous are the

numerous plants of hemp-nettle with pale purple labiate flowers and calyx teeth so long and stiff as to be almost prickly. Hemp-nettle is typically a plant of arable and disturbed ground, but there were several common wetland plants which I had not previously seen along this part of the river, such as bur marigold, water pepper and the tiny marsh yellowcress. A red admiral butterfly sailed over the pool and flew strongly away over the treetops. It is a pleasant water but subject to too much disturbance to attract waterfowl, and very different from the old pool which stretched from bank to bank and contained several willow-green islands on which waterfowl could nest in safety. One of our local floral rarities was the great spearwort, with its huge buttercup-yellow flowers on long stems, which used to grow in great abundance round a small, long-disused reservoir, at least until 1977. A few days ago we walked to see the spearwort again but, alas, it had completely disappeared. It is a scarce plant in Cheshire, and *Newton's*

Flora records it from only thirteen of the 110 grid-squares into which the county is divided. Like the giant bellflower it is now, apparently, locally extinct. In a wide pasture a herd of 150–200 dairy cows were grazing, and a large flock of starlings were foraging amongst them, whilst scores of swallows were flying low above the grass. Doubtless both birds were attracted by the insects disturbed by the cattle.

L. P. SAMUELS *5 September 1989*

PEEBLESSHIRE: Due, no doubt, to a complacent domestic attitude which encourages most forms of wildlife short of slugs and rabbits to make use of our largely overgrown garden, we now have a growing mole problem. Moles in small measure are tolerable, but after a summer in which heaps of earth would appear overnight in a fairly confined area on the west side of the lawn they have spread their activities to appear in widely dispersed areas of the garden. Fresh mounds of earth have been thrown up in previously unaffected areas—through the thick gravel bed of the driveway and through the thinner covering of the paths around the house. Mounds have begun to appear on the distant side of the lawn, fully fifty yards away from the first problem area. Reluctant as I am to call in a professional mole trapper, the small advertisements which appear in the local paper for his skills in mole control and prevention are beginning to look increasingly attractive to me, for my amateur attempts to confine them have clearly failed. Their nuisance-value is considerably increased by our superannuated chickens, which scratch the fresh mounds of earth for worms and grubs and thereby spread a mix of soil and stone over several square yards. Until this recent extension of their range, my control had seemed adequate. When the mounds spread too far I treated each hole, after removing the soil heap, with a generous measure of a powerful and malodorous domestic antiseptic fluid. This, far more than bottles buried in the soil for the wind-whistle effect, clearly had a discouraging effect on the spread of their territory. But whatever it is that motivates the mole, probably nothing more sophisticated than food supply, has made ours territorially adventurous and an increased nuisance as a result.

COLIN LUCKHURST *28 November 1981*

MACHYNLLETH: The Nature Conservancy Council was pleased to announce a substantial addition to its reserve at Borth Bog on the coast of Wales. Good news, you may say, if you care about the safeguarding of our last surviving wildlife habitats. For this wild and unspoiled stretch of peat—the largest of its kind in lowland Britain—is acclaimed as a wetland of international importance. But there is a very odd twist to this story of apparent triumph, as you can easily observe for yourself if you look across the bog from the main road halfway between

Machynlleth and Aberystwyth. There you will see that a wide agricultural ditch has been excavated with the intention of draining that side of the bog. So we have the farcical situation of a government agency trying to keep a wetland wet and a defiant farmer, unsympath-

etic to conservation, doing his best to dry it out. You may well wonder why we have a Nature Conservancy at all if it is so feeble that it cannot protect its choicest reserves from this sort of attack. Nor is this the only national nature reserve under threat. But let us not despair. Parliament has passed the Wildlife and Countryside Bill. So now perhaps we can sit back in wonder, love and praise as magic influences are spread through the land. Will the new act put fresh sinews into nature conservation? Will it strengthen the security of cherished areas like Borth Bog? Or will it merely create new arguments, new anomalies, new absurdities? We shall see.

WILLIAM CONDRY *21 November 1981*

CHESHIRE: On 5 November, pink campion was still in copious bloom at the wood's edge. The plant has a long flowering season, for it is among the earliest woodland blossoms, and this year I noticed it as early as 19 March. The campions do not seem to have ever been credited with any medicinal properties but a strange superstition was attached to them in the Middle Ages when they were believed to be a complete protection against scorpions. Rembert Dudoens, physician to the Emperor, states that "their vertue is so great that this herbe, only throwen before the scorpions, taketh away their power to do harme".

As we climbed up through the gently sloping wood, we neither saw nor heard a single bird, not even the song of a robin nor the chatter of a magpie. We met two quadrupeds, one all too common and the other very rare. The first was a grey squirrel, which fled up a tree-trunk as we approached, and the second was a charming little schipperke, a dog which I had not seen for many years although, in my childhood, I remember it as quite familiar. It is a Flemish breed which is used as a

guard dog and rat-catcher on the canal boats, and its name, translated into English, is "little skipper". It resembles a Manx cat in that its tail is absent or rudimentary. The schipperke was introduced into England in the mid-nineteenth century. In the wood, a large fallen branch was covered with the pretty little bracket fungus, *stereum hirsutum*, velvety-brown with paler edges. The hazels were already decked with long catkins, although these were, of course, still immature and hard. We had the first hoar-frost of the autumn during the night of 5–6 November.

L. P. SAMUELS *14 November 1989*

OXFORDSHIRE: Whilst on Tresco in the last week of October, I picked up the fresh corpse of a little shrew which at first I took to be of the Pygmy species, but which, on second thoughts, did not look quite right for a specimen of our smallest British mammal—the size was about right, but the ears were more prominent and the tail was decidedly whiskery. With birds and plants to distract my attention, I had forgotten the incident until, a few days later, whilst watching a belated northern wheatear on the golf course on St Mary's, a very lively specimen of the same type ran over the toe of my boot to disappear into the grass at my side. Therefore, back at home, one of my first tasks was to turn to my *Handbook of British Mammals,* to confirm that what I had seen was a little beast peculiar to the Scillies—the Scillonian race of the lesser white-toothed shrew, a species otherwise confined, as a British mammal, to the Channel Islands. I had no sooner done this when, on a walk down to our little town, I picked up the fresh corpse of our largest and most handsome shrew—the elusive water-shrew. It was almost as black as a mole and with fur of a

similar velvety texture, but with almost pure white underparts clearly demarcated from the upper dark fur. Apart from its size and dark coloration, the other diagnostic features—a whiskery "keel" beneath its tail, and similar aids to swimming along its digits—were plainly visible. In spite of the aquatic environment which its name suggests, my last local specimen of this rarely encountered mammal was one which, I am ashamed to confess, I trapped inadvertently whilst trying to eradicate the voles in my garden.

W. D. CAMPBELL *18 November 1981*

THE LAKE DISTRICT: Who, I often wonder, builds all these unnecessary route-cairns in the Lakeland fells? Scores, probably hundreds, of new ones have appeared during the year—most of them

on clearly defined tracks—and a similar proliferation has been going on for years. But, in up to a hundred outings each year, I've never seen anybody actually building one. Youth parties, under well-meaning but quite misguided adult leadership, might be partly responsible; their energies would be far better employed in the demolition on every trip, of a few dozen of the more ridiculous ones. Is it not time for the official discouragement of this practice of cairn-building wherever there are stones to hand and, under responsible supervision, the preservation, or even erection, of the relatively few desirable or necessary cairns in the right places? If this could be done sensibly— a big task to cover all the fell routes in the district—cairns could again assume their proper meaning and importance. At present most of them are quite unnecessary, many of them by their senseless profusion or inaccuracy, confusing, hundreds more rubbish heaps or repositories for unsavoury litter, and the whole thing environmentally wrong. Some years ago a party claimed to have erected 128 "stoutly built cairns" along one mile of the well-scored Nan Bield Pass—one unnecessary cairn every fourteen yards—and I once found scores of new cairns along the Blea Rigg high road to Sergeant Man. More enterprising was the aptly named Gadarene Club, to combat the follow-my-leader mentality, formed by the late P. J. H. Unna, mountaineer and land benefactor. In eighteen months he levelled 300 or 400 ugly piles on merely half a dozen Lakeland fells.

A. HARRY GRIFFIN *16 November 1981*

CHESHIRE: By mid-October, wild flowers were becoming difficult to find and, during a walk along the riverside and through the long, wooded gorge, our score was only nineteen. There was still plenty of rather bedraggled Himalayan balsam on the river banks, as well as a clump of Michaelmas daisy—doubtless from a root carried down by the current—and a few tall plants of hogweed, but the other sixteen were not conspicuous. Perhaps the seven species of fungi which we noticed should be added to this total, for they are the fruiting bodies of plants, just as flowers are. The most welcome were four fine field mushrooms growing in a pasture in which horses were grazing. Unfortunately, one of them was snapped up and swallowed by our five-month-old Lakeland puppy before we could stop him. He has a predilection for toadstools but, so far, they do not seem to have hurt him. On a steep, grassy bank which must, a few weeks ago, have been bright with knapweed and devil's-bit scabious, two small copper butterflies were searching for nectar in the tatty flowers that remained. A crab-apple tree bore a large crop of fruit and the grass below it was scattered with little green apples. There were still plenty of hips, haws and blackberries for the winter thrushes. In the woods, a rotting tree-stump bore a mass of honey toadstools, one of the most destructive of all fungi, and, on the other side, in moss, a colony of the tiny white antler fungus, *Xylaria hypoxylon*, a ponderous name for such a pretty, delicate plant. A flock of long-tailed tits were searching through a tall unkept hedge and we watched a sparrowhawk chasing one of our too abundant magpies, which escaped from its pursuer by diving into a densely foliaged tree.

L. P. SAMUELS *24 October 1989*

OXFORDSHIRE: I have always endeavoured, in these weekly pieces, to be meticulously truthful, so several times (in more mobile, pre-accident days) I have left my typewriter and gone to The Forest to

AUTUMN

confirm that something was in bloom, in song, or on the wing: I therefore (being stumped for a theme) have no reservation in describing a recent train of thought which occurred in the intermediate state between consciousness and sleep. I decided that LIFE was no longer worth living—particularly in view of the neglected state of my garden, which was once voted equal first as the best kept in our little town, and the fact that I could no longer visit the usual sites, either by foot or by car, for inspiration for my Diaries. The most appropriate remedy (in the absence of sleeping pills, which I do not possess) seemed to be the berries of a plant which was the subject of my introduction to the Linnean system of plant nomenclature for, over eighty years ago, at the still-extant colony, Dad pointed it out in pedantic Victorian fashion with, "Now look, Willie, this is *Atropa belladonna*—deadly nightshade—and if you ate three or four of these black berries they would kill you." Having decided that, by some means or other, I would get a botanical friend to take me to the site (provided that the apparently immune pheasants and blackbirds had not scoffed the berries first) I was suddenly pulled up by the thought— but what about your *Guardian* piece which you have to write tomorrow? And so the final solution came to nought. Many letters from readers, including no less than ten expressing interest in my recent piece about old apple varieties, supplied flattering encouragement to carry on and, above all, the arrival next day of two of my converts to an interest in natural history in their teenage about forty years ago, to spend several hours digging and cleaning a weedy plot. Since I write this on my eighty-seventh birthday, having received many letters and cards (the latter mainly of birds or flowers), phone calls and visitors, I have to realise that LIFE is still worth living.

W. D. CAMPBELL *11 November 1992*

WINTER

WINTER

WEARDALE, CO. DURHAM: We could see snow flurries advancing over the fell tops across the valley and were glad to reach the shelter of the trees. No sooner were we amongst them than a sudden storm of tiny hailstones swept towards us, like a grey mist. The sound of the approaching curtain of ice crystals pattering on the carpet of dead, dry leaves was like a long, drawn-out hiss, soft at first but increasingly malevolent as the brief storm enveloped us. There was nothing for it but to cower in the lee of a large, decayed beech until the hail subsided. Miniature balls of ice ricocheted from branches, piled up on top of cushions of moss and filled crevices in the cankered bark. On the ground soft, gelatinous folds of yellow brain fungus, *Tremilla mesenterica*, that erupted from the flaking bark of rotting branches, began to fill with hail. The tree was in terminal decay; it had already shed branches and above my head small clusters of *Oudsmansiella mucida*, the porcelain fungus, sprouted from the bark all the way to the crown. I could just reach the caps of the lowest group; smooth, slimy and translucent, clammy and cold to the touch. Most of the surrounding trunks were in advanced stages of decrepitude, pitted by the attacks of foraging woodpeckers and hollowed by fungi. A dying tree may be a marvellous habitat for various forms of wildlife, but it is

121

a melancholy, lingering, undignified end to such a stately organism, as fungal hyphae creep beneath the bark and dissolve away the living tissues. For a few springs yet our sheltering tree might throw out slim branches of fresh green leaves, unless a gale administers the *coup de grâce*. The hail began to peter out and as sunset left a faint glow amongst the clouds on the western horizon we worked our way along the slippery path towards the road, the car and a revitalising flask of hot coffee.

PHIL GATES *6 December 1990*

THE LAKE DISTRICT: After the worst and wettest autumn for years the first sizeable snowfalls heralded a complete change in the weather—hard frost, unbroken sunshine and picture-postcard views. Overnight winter had arrived and magically the beckoning fells loomed closer and, with the snow, seemed twice as high. Not enough snow yet for skiing or climbing but perfect for the familiar round of the Coniston fells. Near the Banishead stone circle I chatted with a farmer getting down the last of his sheep, the dogs scampering down the snow ledges on the little crags with holiday abandon. Yes, he agreed, a "turble clarty back-end", but today what a morning! A steepish snow slope, topped by the beginnings of a cornice, led interestingly to Brown Pike with its superb view of the long, wooded length of Dunnerdale and the battlemented Scafells, etched boldly in white and grey against the bright blue sky. Smoke curled lazily from unseen cottage chimneys in distant woodlands, purple tarns glistened on the lower fells, sunlit sands reached out far away to the glittering sea and the vapour trail of an aircraft crept in a slow arc high over Helvellyn. Sandwiches were eaten in a sunny belvedere, sheltered from the wind by a rock outcrop, just below Goats' Hause. The tarn, edged with snow, looked by contrast even blacker than usual; the soaring white face of the Old Man appeared almost alpine. And from the Brim Fell ridge Coniston might have been a Swiss lakeside town, sparkling in the sunlight. Far to the south the sun touched a window or a car windscreen somewhere near Morecambe Bay and the signal was semaphored to me high up in the snows.

A. HARRY GRIFFIN *4 December 1978*

MACHYNLLETH: This week I have been reading with huge enjoyment the manuscript journals of a lady naturalist who used to live in these parts. There is nothing like old diaries for giving us vivid colour snaps of the past and no matter where I open these chronicles there is always something of interest, whether it is about mammals, birds, insects, wildflowers or simply the weather. As so often happens with diaries, some of her entries have become precious snippets of history. Read, for instance, what she wrote the day she went across to the little island of St Tudwal, which is just off the coast west of Pwllheli. Today it is a somewhat birdless island, but that is not how she experienced it on 26 May 1930:

> As we got near we could see thousands of puffins circling round. The air was thick and the sea black with them. The ground was riddled with their burrows. They soon got used to us and settled only five yards away. Some were billing each other like love birds. Others had fierce fights and rolled over and over down the slope.

It is sad to report today that this great commune of puffins has long since vanished. Our diarist's enthusiasms are wide. A few days after her adventure among the puffins she is at a lakeside near Tywyn. It is hot and thundery and she finds 'the shallows alive with minnows, the cock fish brilliantly coloured with green and red gills'. On another occasion she nets ten-spined sticklebacks, newts and great water beetles out of a ditch near Barmouth. At Harlech she climbs the Roman steps and stalks close to a herd of wild goats. She devotes another day to making a list of the alpine plants growing on one of the cliffs of Cader Idris. Her diaries span the years from 1912 to 1975 and so far I have merely dipped into them. To read them all from end to end is something I think I will have to leave till the long dark evenings of next winter.

WILLIAM CONDRY *26 February 1994*

SOMERSET: We have had crisp, bright, frosty conditions on the last two Saturdays for the nearby legs of the Wessex Grand Prix Carnival

Circuit, at Castle Cary. By seven in the evening rows of eager tiny children, wrapped in blankets and topped by bobble-hats, were sucking toffee-apples in ad hoc grandstands. At Wincanton, the sloping bank of the churchyard, on the bend, is the favoured spot. We

had a preview of one of the local floats. It was made up of one long and one short trailer, hauled by a big farm tractor. It measured a shade longer than a cricket pitch. It had 3,000 light bulbs, fired by the big generator at the back. Twenty-five to thirty people make up the club, which, all year round, in a farmer's barn, prepares this float—theme, design, music, lights, costumes—for the new season. It costs £3,000 to get it on the road. And it is just one of five or six giants of amazing sophistication. They compete for prizes in several categories: Best Overall Float, Tableau, Feature on Vehicle and so on. There are family categories, juvenile categories, classes for Masquerade and Masquerade with Wheels. Four teams of majorettes pranced, pirouetted, and twirled their batons. The route was lined in places, six deep. Through big front windows of the Castle Cary Red Cross Hall you could see senior citizens getting a good view from the warm inside and sipping cups of tea. There are non-competitive participants—police, fire brigade, ambulance service, the Wessex Queen of Queens and her entourage. The firemen put ladders up to top windows and climbed up to collect donations. Three marching bands competed with amplified sound from the floats. Entries numbered 1 to 84 at Castle Cary and 1 to 65 at Wincanton. Many of those who made up these hour-long nose-to-wheel processions will go on to join the Bridgwater Circuit. Bridgwater's carnival is the biggest of all.

JOHN VALLINS *2 November 1993*

OXFORDSHIRE: I have just succeeded, at my first attempt, in making some crab-apple jelly with the true acerbic tang—unlike a friend who had made some from the abundant crops now fallen beneath hedgerow trees, only to find that the end-product was pretty flavourless. The fact is that, although any wild apples are loosely termed "crabs", the genuine article is far outnumbered by "self-setters" from cultivated varieties. Thus, of four specimens in the bottom near my house which is now a Community Nature Reserve, only one, with small long-stemmed yellow fruits, has the requisite mouth-drying effect on the palate. Of the others, one, with larger fruits than the average crab, bears fruits which are acceptably sweet, whilst another, which I sampled before my newly planted garden specimens began to bear, cooks as frothily as a Bramley. The fourth specimen is the most obvious offspring of a cultivar, for its large, conical yellow fruits are typical codlins—and pretty flavourless. Since cultivated varieties must outnumber genuine wildings by many hundreds to one, it is inevitable that cross-pollination will distribute more genes of orchard varieties than of our native crabs—but what of the vectors of the pips? Thrown-away apple-cores are one obvious source, and although I have one ornamental crab, grown from a pip, with fruits only slightly larger than haws, which can be swallowed whole by fieldfares, dispersal through the alimentary tracts of birds is unlikely. But once, when sheltering beneath an old hawthorn during a snowstorm, a marsh-tit flew between my legs, with a small crab-apple held by the stem in its beak, and disappeared momentarily into a hollow between the buttress roots of the tree—and there I found a pyramidal cache of about a dozen similar fruits, stored as a winter reserve.

W. D. CAMPBELL *6 December 1990*

127

NORTHUMBERLAND: Shaftoe crags are an outstanding geological feature which can be seen for miles. Great sandstone boulders cluster one on top of the other. Natural caverns have been created and in one of these Lord Derwentwater is reputed to have hidden whilst rousing local Catholics in 1715 in support of the Pretender. Evidence of Roman colonisation is also apparent for the Romans built a road over the summit of the Crag. Last week I sat on a rock outside Derwentwater's cave and watched for wildlife, although there is little to attract them on this bleak summit. A skein of Canada geese flew overhead making for Sweethope Lough; these imports are on the increase. Two hares slipped through a smoot hole in the drystone wall

and must have disturbed a woodcock because a long-billed, rusty-coloured bird sprang into zigzag flight to weave his way down the bracken-covered slope. I have heard the little goldcrest, Britain's smallest bird, described as the woodcock pilot. This tiny avian, even smaller than the wren, crosses the North Sea in spring and autumn to and from the Scandinavian countries. Perhaps because of their distinctive appearance—olive green with a bright crown above—

goldcrests may have advertised their presence here before the coming of their less brilliantly plumaged fellow travellers, the long-beaked woodcock. The appearance of these two species in autumn at the same time was undoubtedly the reason for the goldcrest's soubriquet of woodcock pilot. Storms, rain, sleet or snow continue unabated. "Can you remember what it was like to go outside in a pair of shoes and without wearing your gloves?" asked our son. So it was with more joy than usual that I noticed the snowdrops appearing along the garden fence. The Christmas roses, as usual, have been marvellous. A blink of sun and I left my bathroom window open. Unfortunately, a pigeon came in and days later I am still finding feathers. And it is true what they say about bowels being loosened by fear. It happens to birds too.

VERONICA HEATH *28 January 1994*

BRANCASTER STAITHE, NORFOLK: It is almost impossible nowadays to travel the coastal road between Cromer and Hunstanton without seeing something of the huge numbers of brent geese that congregate here during the winter months. These birds can look at a distance like some enormous dark organism moving across the fields. At other times elastic skeins, advertising their movements with sharp metallic calls, can extend for hundreds of metres across the skyline. There are approximately 60,000 brent geese in East Anglia and perhaps 100,000 in the country as a whole. This last figure represents just under half the total population breeding in the Soviet tundra and perhaps a quarter of all the world's brents. Yet the species has not always been this abundant. In the 1930s its population crashed, probably because of a combination of over-shooting and a disease that wiped out its main food—a type of marine plant called Zostera. That this Arctic breeder could bounce back from a European total of under 16,500 is a measure of its resilience. Its recovery has brought in its wake problems. Having completed their lengthy migration across northern Europe, brents arrive in this country from October onwards. Initially the birds feed on Zostera and other green algae in the intertidal zone, moving on to the saltmarsh once these food sources have been depleted. Then, when the saltmarsh plants, like samphire, are also exhausted, the geese move inland on to pasture and winter-sown arable crops. Their persistent grazing can cause substantial damage, in some instances reducing the grain yield by up to fifteen per cent. One solution has been found in the Ministry of Agriculture's set-aside scheme and the Countryside Commission's Countryside Premium scheme. Areas of pasture are made attractive for the geese and they are allowed to graze there, while some method of scaring keeps them off the rest of the crops.

MARK COCKER *10 December 1990*

LINCOLN'S HIGH WOLDS: There is nowhere quite like the great chalk country of Lincolnshire. At any season the empty spaces evoke another age; the lack of human population is remarkable in the twentieth century. The highest point in all that huge county is a flat-topped spur above Normanby le Wold. Its 550 feet hardly overtops lots of other brows in this part, and there is no footpath crossing it. Not far away, though, a path wanders down to the north into the quite dramatic valley drained by the Nettleton Beck. On the hillside near by stands the former Roman settlement we now call Caistor, a quiet country town largely overlooked by the world. Little more than a mile to the north rises the 128-feet Pelham's Pillar, erected in 1840 to commemorate the planting of twelve million trees by Lord Yarborough on his Brocklesby estate. The plantings, now at or beyond maturity, sweep round in a great arc across the gentle arable country to Great Limber village and on to Brocklesby. Great Limber lies on the high road to Grimsby, and towering on its roadside tumulus mound, but hidden by trees, is what Pevsner called "Lincolnshire's finest building after Lincoln Cathedral". The Brocklesby Mausoleum was erected by the first baron, C. A. Pelham, for his young wife Sophia after her death in 1786. It is one of James Wyatt's most successful buildings in a quite unexpected situation, with tree-top views and a clear vista to Brocklesby Hall one and a half miles away across the cornlands. If you walk that way, northwards through the narrow ribbon of woods towards the great house, you will come upon a walnut tree planted here in February 1938 by Countess Yarborough to commemorate the thirty million trees inserted in the Brocklesby and Manby Woods since 1787: an unsung achievement by unassuming landlords in an overlooked corner.

ROGER A. REDFERN *15 December 1990*

CHESHIRE: Having succumbed to a heavy cold, my birdwatching over the Christmas holiday has been restricted to watching the

comings and goings at the bird table and nut feeders in the garden. I've been very pleased to see that the wire nut baskets I bought recently as "squirrel proof" have defied all attempts, so far, to tear them apart. A new feature this winter is a seed feeder which automatically tops up two small dishes as they become empty. This proved an attraction one morning when two of the local collared doves brought a friend with them. I like to think it was a "Christmas dove", but after some research I came to the conclusion that it was a diamond dove, smaller than its companions, about two-thirds their size, with a large, bright red eye ring contrasting with blue-grey plumage of head and shoulders, and both wings being covered with a pattern of fine white dots. The diamond dove is a native of the hot interior of Australia, and I recall watching a small group drinking from a shallow pool near Ayer's Rock in late 1991, with the temperature over 100°F and rising. On that December day in the garden it was hovering around zero and falling. Having almost certainly escaped from captivity, I hope my bird found its way back to a warm, friendly aviary. Amongst all the activity around the feeders, the song thrush has been a very infrequent visitor. In past years it has not been unusual to hear one in song at Christmas time. It isn't a showy, aggressive bird like its relative the blackbird, but tends to stand back from the fray until others have finished and then move in quietly to feed on what is left. As I finished these notes the squirrel was back at the nut baskets—hind feet clinging to the clothes line, front feet gripping the wire mesh of the holder, and teeth gnawing away quite viciously—but it still couldn't make much progress.

J. M. THOMPSON *5 January 1993*

HAMSTERLEY FOREST, CO. DURHAM: Attitudes to conifers oscillate between approval and antipathy depending on the season. At this time of year millions of infant Norway spruces are welcomed into homes; at other times the sight of regimented plantations of juvenile examples of the same species is less popular. I have reservations about aspects of commercial forestry, but in this forest there are some handsome, well-thinned, maturing specimens of the humble Christmas tree which must be over seventy feet tall and are a pleasure to walk amongst. Their lower branches have been removed, leaving sticky trickles of resin oozing from the wounds; today, freezing and windless, the fruity smell hung in the still air between the trees. This year they produced a particularly fine crop of long, spindle-shaped cones that now lie ankle-deep on the forest floor. Many have been worked by crossbills, with the cone scales split cleanly down the middle by their scissor-like beaks. Some, gnawed by red squirrels, are

133

discarded around tree stumps that the squirrels use as feeding tables. The decaying stumps have a characteristic flora of mosses and liverworts, with neat circular lime-green patches of the leafy liverwort *Lophocolea* that have an almost luminous glow in the shade beneath the trees. We have often disturbed woodcock sheltering here and this afternoon was no exception. The combination of frozen snow, a heavy cone crop, and gales had snapped the tops from some trees, sending them crashing to the forest floor. It was while we were pulling cones from one of these, for Christmas decorations, that we put up a woodcock crouching below it. So perfect was its camouflage that we must have been only a yard away when it burst out from below the broken branches and zigzagged to safety through the trees.

PHIL GATES *28 December 1990*

OXFORDSHIRE: Before the latest set-back to my mobility, I had gathered the choicest specimens of fist-sized Bramley Seedlings and dual-purpose Allington Pippins without having to use ladder or steps, since many years ago I had grafted them, in preparation for retirement, on dwarfing stocks. But the standard trees—Egremont Russet, Laxton's Exquisite and Sturmer Pippin 6—have remained unharvested. The second of these, an early ripener, was not worth picking, since all the sizeable specimens had been punctured by tits, and only a few visiting children enjoyed those available. The Sturmer, a very late developer, was mistakenly grafted on to a stronger stock, and was left to await harvesting until the first week in December. When I returned from hospital in the middle of that month, many were still on the tree. Such was the firmness of their attachment that birds could reduce them to mere shells and cores without dislodging them and it was interesting to note that apart from the jackdaws, thrush species and tits which were consuming the pulp, greenfinches were only interested in the exposed pips. Severe frosts in mid-December (with minimum of 17°F on two consecutive nights) brought down the remnant of the crop, rendering the windfalls unfit for use by friends who normally glean them. But they are still acceptable to a wide variety of birds. From the window I have seen blackbirds, fieldfares, song thrushes, redwings and starlings, with the occasional jackdaw, tit or greenfinch swarming on the apple-strewn ground. One bird which disappeared before I had focused my binoculars was, I felt sure, a winter-visiting blackcap—two such individuals were known to have visited the tree last winter.

W. D. CAMPBELL *15 January 1992*

MACHYNLLETH: On a farm here half a century ago a woman made a garden. She had it fenced and at each side of the gate she planted a rowan tree. Then, when these two trees had grown taller than herself, she twisted their branches together to form an arch over the gate. In so doing she was following the ancient belief that rowans keep away evil spirits. Years later, when she went to live elsewhere, no one bothered about the garden and it eventually disappeared along with its fence and

135

its gate. But the two rowans have survived, still with their branches intertwined. The woman's son has the farm now, a man with respect for country tradition. He has inherited not only the two rowans but also the beliefs that go with them. He therefore looks after the trees and keeps their arch neatly shaped. Not that he would ever admit to believing in rowan superstitions. You cannot be a respectable churchgoer and go in for pagan ritual (except at Christmas). When the time comes for this man to leave the farm his son will take over and my guess is that the rowans will go on being cared for. Meanwhile, perhaps the father will have built himself a bungalow to retire to. If so, I bet he will plant a rowan at each side of his gate, whatever the vicar may think. Who knows, perhaps people will still be making rowan-tree arches when Christianity has long been forgotten?

WILLIAM CONDRY *30 December 1978*

NORTHUMBERLAND: The village we live in is small and picturesque. It hosts a Lutyens manor house, a church school with less than thirty pupils, a church, a shop and a blacksmith's shop and a village hall. Commuters have infiltrated and bought up, and done up, the old stone cottages but we have accepted this as inevitable. It is a pity they do not patronise the church or the shop or the activities in the hall. However we are grateful for the one or two souls who do support us. Now a new and fearful horror has ignited our community to indignation. We have one farm in our short village street and the farmer is selling the house and planning permission is being sought to convert the farm buildings into fourteen houses and several flats. The noise and the mud and the congestion around the one narrow farm entrance whilst building is going on will be appalling. I do not want any more fast cars rushing past while I walk our dogs, ride my old horse, or push a grandchild in the pram to the forge to see the farrier at work. Neither do the pensioners, several of whom take several minutes to cross the village street. When the nights draw in, out come the torches, but will a motorist bound for the fleshpots of Newcastle notice them? The village folk are themselves heading for whist in the village hall, warmed by a proper fire. Freezing cold and heavy rain never daunt them, so it will take more than heavy traffic to put them off. Thefts have increased ten-fold in ten years. Our newcomers have clearly got possessions worth pilfering but the burglars prey on us, too. The parish council is fighting the planning application on our behalf but I have a sinking feeling that we shall lose our village identity and be swallowed up.

VERONICA HEATH 7 *December 1990*

CHESHIRE: Although the sun was rapidly melting the hoar-frost, lawns and pastures were glittering. But the frost could not have been very severe, for the path through the wood was still soft and slippery with mud. A tiny bird was searching through the branches of a hawthorn. It was obviously a coal marsh or willow tit, but it had no white patch on its nape, so the coal, was eliminated. The marsh and willow tits are not separable in the field, except at very close quarters, save by their call-notes, and this bird was silent until we were on the point of giving up when it uttered the thin triple call which identified it as a willow tit. The "pitchuu" of the marsh tit is unmistakable. In a manured field, a small flock of *turdidae* were foraging. We hoped that they might be fieldfares but binoculars revealed them as only mistle thrushes.

On a birch stump several specimens of the false oyster-fungus, *pleurotus serotinus*, were growing. It is not a very common fungus and is not edible. Its cap is olive-grey with none of the deep blue or almost purple lustre of the true oyster-fungus. In grass, under trees, solitary as they usually are, was a tall toadstool, *pluteus cervinus*, with a dark brown cap and a pale stem darkly streaked. Along some twenty yards on both sides of a lane, the mushrooms *agaricus vaporarius* were abundant, their caps pale brown with numerous large scales of a darker colour. This was a remarkable find, for Roger Phillips's *Mushrooms and Other Fungi* states it is rare and edible, but our specimen exactly matched the excellent photograph in his book. The mushroom of commerce is *agaricus campestris*.

The mention, in a recent Diary, of a red admiral butterfly on the wing as late as 9 November has brought letters from two readers reporting the insect in Cheshire, one on the 13th at Frodsham and one on the 13th at Warrington.

L. P. SAMUELS *5 December 1989*

THE RADCLIFFE INFIRMARY, NUFFIELD II, OXFORD: This is the piece which should have appeared on 27 November, but, despite posting six days earlier, it never reached its destination. It was written from the John Radcliffe Hospital. Now, after more than three months,

139

I write once more from this address, having had a setback (lung trouble and a slight stroke). But in the intervening good spells I got about, and was pleased to receive many visitors on my eighty-sixth birthday. Another ring of the doorbell did not herald, as I expected, more well-wishers, by my friend the smallholder from just up the lane, obviously excited by the news which he brought. Whilst picking sprouts in pouring rain, he had been accompanied by an apparent family party of pheasants, but although the assumed parents had the normal plumage of cock and hen, the seven full-grown youngsters were all white. In an area where thousands of pheasants are reared, an odd albino specimen is not unusual, but a whole brood seems exceptional. The reared birds are virtually orphans, not forming family groups, so that it seems as if its white family was a natural wild brood in parental care. But I still cannot account for the presence of the cock bird, for normally this polygamist fathers several broods, and does not share parental care. It cannot have been beaters and shooters which caused this party to seek shelter, for it was a Sunday; probably the torrential rain had caused the family to realise that Brussels sprouts offered drier cover than the ubiquitous oilseed rape. Care here (the John Radcliffe) has been of the expected high standard—but this time the traditional lassies were aided by male nurses—equally patient, cheerful and efficient.

W. D. CAMPBELL *11 December 1991*

RICHMOND PARK: Real winter weather: rain that pours down, tempestuous winds, sudden pauses for washed blue sky, low sun and flying clouds. All this I associate with west Wales. Hogmanay produced a real corker. The rain fell with such wild abundance that the

strongest of the many Welsh words for rain was inadequate. The younger of the two labradors hurled herself into the farm pond with trusting abandon. She came up paddling rapidly, retrieved the stick and then shook water all around. I used the occasion to try out a present: one of those long waxed coats. I arrived home dry. But this year London has "real" weather. Freezing temperatures turned all the watery places into ice. We heard the wonderful echo of stones hurtling across frozen water. A black swan in the Isabella Plantation struggled with ice too thin to hold, but too substantial to be easily swept aside. Finally she made it to clear water and moved off with the triumphant majestry that swans command. However, spring is putting out her feelers. Midwinter wych-hazel trees are all in delicate, fragrant blossom. Even with each branch and flower capped with frozen snow the scent remains strong. Warm days will return. The cold dead grasses will be renewed. Delicate damselflies will charm our eyes. Now when the storms abate you hear the clear song of thrushes and blackbirds. In the garden male blackbirds carefully shadow females. A greater spotted woodpecker turned up to try his luck with the tit feeder. The smaller birds had gone for the sunflower seeds leaving the woodpecker free to peck the peanuts before returning to the old pear tree to tap for grubs. His jaunty figure and colourful coat—white, buff, glossy black and crimson—stood out against the bare tree. The more weather wages the more I enjoy it. Now time takes me by the shadow of my hand: I'll be writing more from the wild weather and airy spaces of Pembrokeshire in future.

AUDREY INSCH *22 January 1994*

MACHYNLLETH: It was not till I came over the rise that shelters our house from the west that I realised that the gale blowing on Sunday afternoon was a greater wind than I had ever known. This was not because it knocked me over three times in three minutes but because there before me lay several big pine trees which had stood isolated in the estuary winds for maybe a century. As I turned away to see how the nearby woodland was getting on, another great pine hit the ground where I had been standing ten seconds before. I found the sheltered side of the wood was comparatively quiet but as I got near the top of the ridge I came up into a different world just as the wind began to find its greatest strength. Here for the first time in my life, and I hope the last, I was in a wood with trees crashing all round me. Many were larches and spruces but as the gale increased even oaks and sycamores, the very symbols of stability, began to fall like skittles. By four o'clock the worst was over and I could go round counting the fallen. The hard woods were on the ground in hundreds, the conifers uncountable. Many of the stricken oaks I had known so long they were among my oldest friends. That some were trees nearly two centuries old is evidence that no such wind has blown just here in a very long time. Next day I found that it had been a freakishly local sort of tornado. For in the very next parish hardly a twig had gone off a tree anywhere.

WILLIAM CONDRY *19 December 1981*

THE LAKE DISTRICT: From the tall beacon column on the summit of Thornthwaite Crag this sunny, frosty day the views were quite magical—breathtaking clarity to the north but, to the south, a double temperature inversion that painted the scene with all the subtleties of a Chinese painting. Mist hovered in all the little valleys between Threshthwaite Mouth and Windermere and, perhaps 1,000 feet higher, another bank of cloud hung halfway up the fells, with further horizontal layers higher in the sky in roughly parallel progression. All this fleecy whiteness was illuminated from above by blazing sunlight with ridges and fell tops poking through here and there, piled above each other, while near and distant waters, above and below the cotton-wool carpets, sparkled and danced across the picture. The flat top of Ingleborough was just one tiny section of hillside hanging high in the sky with other bits of fells, becks or woodlands scattered lower down the picture and the white, sunlit strips of cloud floating in between. In comparison the view to the north was as clear as any I can remember with the ridges of Blencathra sharp and distinct as if cut out of cardboard. The switchback line of the Coniston Fells, Bowfell, the Scafells and Helvellyn further to the north-west crowded the western horizon, black against the setting sun and, eastwards, High Street and its satellites looked within a stone's throw. We had come up the shadowed and icy Threshthwaite Cove from Hartsop, returning in the sunlight over Gray Crag. Hounds were out in Deepdale and we were glad that a fox we had spotted scampering up Brock Crags had got well clear. He reminded me of a fox I once watched for a quarter of an hour while he leisurely climbed the snowbound zigzags of Thornthwaite Crag unaware he was in full view from a perch on the Caudale Moor crags. People met on our round said they had seen thirteen red deer from the heights above Martindale. We had seen a buzzard soaring over Pasture Beck and a pair of ravens doing aerial gymnastics above Raven Crag. Another interesting encounter on the top of Thornthwaite Crag was with a couple who proudly identified Blencathra as Helvellyn and had no idea of the name of the fell they had ascended.

A. HARRY GRIFFIN *11 January 1993*

WAINFLEET, LINCOLNSHIRE: Never before have I found a rare bird so easy to observe. Only seconds after our arrival, and from several kilometres away, it stood out on these flat, dark, sodden

coastal fields like a miniature snowman. Snowy owl, the second
largest owl in western Eurasia, is a truly magnificent creature. This
bird, a male, was pure white apart from brown tips to some of the
wing, mantle and tail feathers. The slightly larger female can stand
two-thirds of a metre tall, while her wingspan is a metre and a half.
Both sexes have large piercing yellow eyes and rather catlike faces. In
fact on Shetland the species is known as the "cat owl". This
northernmost archipelago is the only regular site in the British Isles for
the usually high Arctic snowy. From 1967 to 1975 a single pair (which

in 1973 became a *ménage à trois*) reared a total of sixteen young. Since the latter date, unfortunately, females have continued to return but without the male. It is hard to believe that such a conspicuous bird can ever be difficult to observe. Yet on the Shetland island of Fetlar they apparently blend in well with the open, boulder-strewn moorland. Remaining immobile for long periods, the owls can easily be overlooked as just another pale rock. For the first hour of observation our bird was fully justifying the snowy's reputation for inertia. And for all its rarity and spectacular appearance, watching a completely stationary white object from several hundred metres away in the middle of a windswept field eventually began to pall. I was even tempted to abandon it briefly and follow a short-eared owl as it hunted along the field margin. Then suddenly all changed. The great white wings opened and it cruised off, swooping unsuccessfully at some panic-stricken partridge. Then, rather unexpectedly, he landed only a few metres from a large hare. For a few comical seconds, the mammal (a potential prey species for the owl) seemed to blink at the pale apparition in disbelief, before beating a hasty retreat.

MARK COCKER *7 January 1991*

MACHYNLLETH: After my annual stroll round the precipice walk
near Dolgellau, I found I still had time for another frolic. A steep
heathery slope offered an irresistible scramble to a rocky summit that
had views of mountains all round. Along the south was the whole
range of Cader Idris streaked with white from end to end. There was
even more snow on Aran in the east but none at all on Rhinog in the
west. I sat on a lichen-covered rock enjoying the near-silence of the
hills. All I could hear was the swishing of the wind through the long,
white, dead grasses, one of the loveliest sounds of winter. All about me

on the summit I was delighted to see copious traces of the folk of the
Iron Age, always my favourite prehistoric people simply because I so
enjoy climbing to their hill forts, which are so abundant on the lesser
hills of Wales and are all such fine viewpoints. I was pleased to find not
only the tumbled walls of once massive defences but the foundations
of several Iron Age houses still clear to see though their occupants
abandoned them perhaps 2,000 years ago. I like to think of those hardy
tribes keeping a watchful eye on the hills all round and on the valleys
below. Their lives were probably often full of fear yet surely there

must have been tranquil days when they enjoyed the panoramas just as much as we do today? But even had there been no hill fort, no traces of the Iron Age people, I should still treasure the day for its spectacular weather. It was a December afternoon when inky clouds and brilliant gleams were doing wonderful things, bringing moments of great drama as the sun peeped through slits in the clouds, and creating oases of brilliant illumination that contrasted theatrically with the blue-black shadows that engulfed some of the mountain tops.

WILLIAM CONDRY *1 January 1994*

NORTHUMBERLAND: The sea-coal man's pony on Lynemouth links, standing hock-deep in the sea, while his master raked for coal in the shingle on the ebbing tide, uncharacteristically took a step or two into the waves and must have found the sandbank disappear beneath his hoofs. Within seconds, we saw that the animal was swimming strongly out to sea, taking his flat cart with him. The coalie man watched helplessly as his livelihood looked in imminent danger of disappearing in the freezing January waves. Those of us who were exercising dogs and collecting driftwood on the beach watched the drama in fascinated horror. Rescue services were alerted, but before they arrived the staunch little pony had revised his sense of direction and abandoned his bid to reach Norway. We watched him swim a wide arc and then head back towards the links. It was a mercy that the cart did not become waterlogged and drag the pony down. The coalie man told me that the incident was unprecedented and that they could not recall a drowning involving their ponies. A few of these ponies are kept in sheds during severe frost such as we experienced here early this month, but most are hobbled or tethered and live on the bleak dunes. They all look content and well fed, and thrive on the hard work and the beneficial salt water continually washing hoofs and tendons. With hay at a premium this year, it is fortunate that the sea-coal families have traditional scythes and rakes and have kept up the habit of making hay themselves from grass verges and common land at Cresswell and Lynemouth. They stook the grass after drying and use their flat carts to transport it to winter shelter. The local newspaper advertises sea coal now at £4 a bag and there are plenty of customers.

VERONICA HEATH *10 January 1986*

HYDE PARK: The cold clutches everything. Squirrels finding themselves absent-mindedly still awake and supposedly alert sit forlornly about on trees, under bedraggled brambles—anywhere that seems likely to provide shelter. Puffed-out wood pigeons droop on the higher branches. Even some of the coots have abandoned the clatter and squabble of the food fight to flop on the bruised grass to do nothing but highlight the frozen grey of the ground with their black and white. Colour is difficult to find. Buds will quickly provide it when the cold lifts, but the vibrant crimson of the dogwood stands on its own. Where the ice has been discouraged the birds dash around assured of piles of food. We were accompanied by a Dutch friend who had been spending time skating. In Holland the newspapers print details of the local skating tours. You turn up with your skates and have a round trip with fellow enthusiasts—30, 50 and more kilo-

metres. We looked at the board telling us the ice was unsafe, we could be fined £50 for setting foot on it, and wondered if it ever would be allowed to be safe. The Serpentine of my youth was a small loch in Perthshire by Loch Ochtertyre. The head boy told the headmaster, "Sir, the ice is bearing" and we had a holiday. Every bicycle carrying at least two people, we swarmed icewards and skated into the dark. "Proud and exulting like an untired horse That cares not for his home . . . So through the darkness and the cold we flew", as Wordsworth does in *The Prelude*. On this Serpentine one little boy in a duffle coat ventured forth, completely lost to the cries of "Oy!" and the presence of the scarlet ladder leaning on the fence, so entranced was he by the experience.

AUDREY INSCH *1 March 1986*

OXFORDSHIRE: A recent Diary from the North-East mentioned the widely held belief that a hard, frosty winter was beneficial to subsequent crops since it killed off pests. Experience based on many hard winters and many years of gardening, in my case enhanced by my annual search for one of the main classes of plant pests—aphids—to use

for bait in my bird cage-traps, has led me to believe that this optimistic opinion is entirely fallacious. Indeed, I can think of some ways in which prolonged frosts favour the survival of underground insect pests such as leather-jackets, wireworms and the pupae of various moths whose caterpillars are cut-worms. The frozen crust of the soil, even if only a few inches deep, ensures the safety of the pests below from probing beaks of rooks and starlings. But there now exists scientific evidence that freezing is not necessarily lethal either to minute invertebrate pests such as aphids, or the even tinier spores of fungal diseases. Samples of such aerial plankton (including non-pests such as tiny spiders) taken from a great height where the thin atmosphere is well below freezing, on being returned to ground-level in an apparently dead, frozen-solid state, rapidly thaw and become actively alive. But the best illustration of this ability of some animal life to survive being frozen solid occurred in the exceptionally prolonged spell of hard frost during the winter of 1962–3. On a bank in the corner of my garden lay a sheet of corrugated iron, and I lifted it in search of any items which might be of value to my hungry thrushes and robins. But what I found was a mass of hundreds of garden snails stuck together, and all in their sealed-up dormant condition. I took about half a dozen into school to show my class and fortunately did not stress the apparent beneficial effect of the weather. The arithmetic lesson then proceeded, but after about ten minutes the class appeared to lose application to their sums, and all eyes were directed to my desk—it was crawling with active snails.

W. D. CAMPBELL *26 January 1994*

WINTER

HOPE SCAR, NORTH YORKSHIRE: The view from this rocky precipice in the Stang Forest is awesome. The cliff edge is 1,000 feet above the distant flood plain of the River Tees, which extends as a patchwork of fields, farms and small woodlands below. Away to the north-west lies bleak Bowes Moor; far to the east, the Cleveland Hills and the smoking chimneys and cooling towers of Teesside industry are just visible on the horizon. Today the spectacle was especially exhilarating because the base of the clouds was almost level with the edge of the cliff. As they raced overhead the shafts of sunlight that pierced them swept like spotlights over the fields and woodlands below. This is an excellent spot for watching birds of prey, as large areas of the Stang have been felled over the last few years, leaving acres of tussocky grass which provide a perfect habitat for small mammals. On several occasions we have been able to watch short-eared owls quartering the open ground below the scree slope. Today we were even luckier. A buzzard drifted over the trees to our right, swooped low over the yellow grass and dark-green blocks of conifers below, and then soared in wide circles. For a moment the pale undersides of its wings were caught in the sunlight, before it disappeared amongst the slate-grey clouds. Buzzards are uncommon on this side of the Pennines, despite the super-abundance of rabbits. This was the first we had seen for many years, and so ranked as a highlight of the Christmas holidays. But the most unusual encounter occurred near our home three days before Christmas, on the winter solstice. A day of unseasonably warm, still weather aroused a nest of wild honey-bees in an old alder. Their foraging fights were futile, but they did provide a portent of spring on the darkest day of winter.

PHIL GATES *9 January 1992*

SOMERSET: Some fifteen years ago, during a very cold winter spell, a Dorsetshire sheep-farmer who was staying with us in Manchester sniffed the air one evening and at once telephoned his shepherd to warn him to get the sheep off the high ground. The next day's news reported many sheep lost in West Country snowdrifts, but his flock was safe.

This year, the plentiful sheep on the slopes and ridges towards Sherborne, including the youngest lambs, look plump, happy and safe enough. At the turn of the year there has been frost and on some days clouds of cold fog have suddenly engulfed whole hills, passing as swiftly to let in the sunshine again, but there has not been the snow to distress the sheep or make the distant sheep-farmer anxious. Back on Christmas day, the south-facing slopes over towards Mere and Wiltshire were damp green, and only a thin mist hung across them; but once over the hilltops, facing north, the fields were frozen white, the trees like a Christmas-card picture and the cattle, when glimpsed through the thickening fog, steaming statues. At Horningsham, the tiny hamlet by the main Longleat gatehouse, visibility was down to fifty yards or so. The Longleat drive runs a straight kilometre to the cattle-grid and twin lakes, frozen solid, that guard the house itself. On either side trees materialised, singly or in twos and threes, out of the white blankness. The eye strained for the familiar outline of the house which at last loomed mysteriously straight ahead. At the same time, eerily, from over on the right, disembodied sounds—strange animal grunts and cries—registered the presence on the estate of more exotic beasts than sheep. At "Heaven's Gate", the notable viewpoint on one rim of the great bowl of Longleat parkland, where seats are placed for enjoyment of the panorama, there was only a precipice and a vertical blanket of grey-white space. Back across the road, a notice of application for planning permission for a "holiday village, pancake house and *jardin des sports*" showed how country landowners diversify these days—not only into golf courses.

JOHN VALLINS *12 January 1993*

BATTERSEA PARK: The freeze was lingering. Here the lake retained enough ice to support squalling groups of river gulls, walking like the stiff-legged marionettes. Some shovellers kept to themselves in a bay where the ice had been broken and they could swim around. Moorhens pattered along the banks, while the coots swithered between ice, water and earth. The island presented a bleak aspect, with trails of smoke circling from it. The old willows have been felled: all have been found to be suffering from disease, decay, instability, or the ravages of age. An 1846 Act of Parliament started the creation of this park from the marshes of old Battersea Fields, helped with the soil removed from the extension of Victoria Dock. Now it is an area of surprising charm and variety. The magnificent avenues of mature planes, giving an impressive experience of the power of massed trees, wind through different habitats designed for man and beast. The unusual is catered for in large aviaries of birds from other countries, dazzling reds and blues in the winter greyness. The strongest native colours are the new forsythia and the faded tangerine of the remaining willow trees. Even the evergreens seemed to be tired of the cold, especially in comparison with the fresh green of the daffodils. By the river there was no protection from the east wind swooping off the water to tear through our coats. We went along to the pagoda that is being built by a group of Japanese Buddhists. The top piece was being lowered into position, an oriental extravagance of gold and blue delicately manoeuvred by a tall crane. When the building is finished, another marvel will be started and we will be able to savour a Japanese garden.

AUDREY INSCH *2 February 1985*

GLOUCESTERSHIRE: A winter as wet as this one makes life additionally stressful for field animals. Our land is not particularly water retentive, most of it slopes and there is run-off, but such has been the quantity of rain that we have some standing water. It is sheep feet which become a problem following prolonged exposure to wet surface conditions. Poor Myfanwy, a two-year-old Black Welsh Mountain ewe was clearly in trouble yesterday morning. She was struggling on three feet with her front left foot unable to carry weight. Being of a sensible disposition she did not panic when we appeared with the sheep seat, the nail clippers and the foot spray. We upended her carefully, for she ought to be two months pregnant, washed and clipped the keratin of all four feet and gave each a precautionary spray against rot. Instant relief for Myfanwy and did I detect a look of gratitude in those dark Celtic eyes? Probably not, but at least she is catchable, unlike the flighty Soays. Which brings me to the hitherto unresolved mystery of Houdini, the Soay ram lamb who fled after a serious battering from his father. Answers on a postcard please, I requested, and the mail brought an untraceable reply with a local postmark to my question: where is he now? Mary, of no recorded address, reported him to be already in her freezer. So I hope he tastes well and, roasted *à point* in the French fashion, he should go very well with a decent claret. Back on the foot front, I imagine that the sodden conditions will force us to do a foot treatment for the entire flock. The only alternative is a long walk over a rough track which will wear down the soft growth. In our first year with sheep when such arcane mysteries were beyond me we had young Robin to do the lot in rapid style with a Stanley knife followed by a night penned on limed sand. He went off to farm in France, enticed by cheaper land and a bigger Euro-subsidy, but at least we learned the technique.

COLIN LUCKHURST 7 *January 1994*

INVERNESS: The headline in the local newspaper ran, "Death of St Kilda's last child" and gave an account of Neil MacKinnon, who had died, aged sixty-one. He was the last child born on St Kilda, four years before the islanders were evacuated to the mainland in 1930. Like many of the St Kildans, he settled first in Lochaline, near Fort William, where the men went to work for the Forestry Commission. This was ironic as most of them had never seen a tree; there is none on their archipelago. It was also a dramatic social change, because for the first time the women were separated from their husbands all day. I had the great pleasure of spending a week last summer with Lachlan MacDonald, who was in his early twenties at the time of the evacuation. We toured the islands by yacht and landed a few times in

Hirta. It was particularly interesting to hear how many mistakes and wrong impressions exist in the growing number of books about the St Kildans. Lachlan was full of stories about the climbs, and pointed out the traditional routes on such crags as Stac Lee and Stac an Armin. He thrilled again at the puffins, gannets and fulmars, and could not understand why I could not let him have a puffin to eat. A few St Kildans go back occasionally; in their old houses they have placed a few round boulders on which they record at each visit their name and the year. Perhaps their feelings about the evacuation can best be summed up by these words from a St Kilda woman, now married in Lewis:

> I should prefer to all the cattle I have got
> To be in St Kilda plucking the guillemot,
> Along with the grey-billed solan goose
> Which snatches the fish from the surface of the current.

RAY COLLIER *31 December 1987*

OXFORDSHIRE: The caterpillar of the deaths' head hawk moth, which I mentioned as having been found during potato-digging in my former Berkshire haunts some months ago, underwent only a brief pupation, and hatched into the adult stage some weeks ago. It was released somewhere in the extreme South-East but I doubt whether it will survive even in this more continental climate. The pupa, buried in soil, had been kept indoors and therefore hatched prematurely. This leads me to wonder about the fate of a chrysalis which I have just discovered indoors—on the wall just inside the front door. At first I was puzzled as to its identity for I had never seen one like it before: sage green with a few minute black dots. From its size and shape I concluded that it was one of the cabbage whites and finally decided that it was the pupa of the small white, which varies from greyish or

159

yellowish to green. In the warmth of the house a premature emergence of the perfect insect is likely and then my assumption will be verified (or disproved—it may turn out to be a green-veined white). But I doubt whether many offspring of the most pestilential of the cabbage butterflies—the large white, which have skeletonised many brassica beds this year—will reappear in the spring. Of the few which escaped my attention just as they hatched from the clusters of eggs many pupated on the rough-cast wall of my house and of these five kept under daily observation were destroyed by ichneumon larvae. This is the usual fate of attempts by the large white to 'be fruitful and multiply' and I consider that it should be mainly regarded as a migratory species, for it is often scarce in spring but suddenly becomes abundant in late summer. I remember one day in early August about forty years ago when, as far as the eye could see, the surface of the sea at Folkestone was twinkling with myriads of large whites approaching just above the waves.

W. D. CAMPBELL *8 January 1992*